C000176130

A

RESOUNDING VOICE

&

Echoes from the Welsh Valleys

AN ANTHOLOGY

by

RAY HARMAN

HORSESHOE PUBLICATIONS
KINGSLEY, WARRINGTON
CHESHIRE

ISBN 1 899310 22 3

First published 1995 by
HORSESHOE PUBLICATIONS
Box 37, Kingsley, Warrington,
Cheshire WA6 8DR

Book cover designed by Cheshire Artist
TRACY WALKDEN

Printed and bound in Great Britain by
ANTONY ROWE LTD
Chippenham, Wiltshire

DEDICATION

I dedicate this collection of my poetic work to my lovely wife, Dot, who typed every one of its words, deciphered my sprawling handwriting and corrected my many mistakes. Without the inspiration of her presence and the unfailing support she has always provided, this book of mine would never have gone to press.

I have known and admired Ray Harman's work for many years.

His work above all is for his people. A celebration of their hopes and dreams. He has the rare gift to paint sad still pictures of a cherished childhood. His acute observations evoke warm, nostalgic memories of a bygone age.

His work is both moving and inspirational and I thoroughly recommend this collection of his poems to all lovers of poetry.

MAX BOYCE

Unlike a novel which has a beginning and an end, the poetry which is always in the heart and mind of Ray Harman is only waiting for the next blank page on which to inscribe the message to those who do perceive and care.

Editor

~~~~~~~~~~~~~~~~~~~

A Poetic assessment of the Verse of Ray Harman by the Editor.

POETRY

What is poetry?
Is it the lilting writing of an educated hand?
Or the passion flamed mind seeking expression?

Not for me, the pretty waters so calm,
But like a torrent, tumbling and roaring,
My spirit must have rein to soar,
To touch the skies, and plunge the depths into despair,
Love, hate, envy, need and compassion are the
Essential composites of poetry that matters,
Loneliness, happiness and fulfilment add
Their spice to the magic brew.

But how can poetry exist without heart or passion?
It is like weak tea, or flat and featureless as a great plain.
Talking pretty words, soon bores those who
Would listen, but, if you feel your poetry
You will inspire those who listen, they will
Feel moved, as they recognise emotions
Within themselves.

The powerful words of the long-dead still inspire
And are enjoyed by the hungry minds
Of those who seek to learn.

In poetry every generation can add its own contribution
To the colourful fabric and tapestry
That is poetry. Ad Infinitum.

A Resounding Voice

INDEX

SOMETIME TOMORROW

The last cage sank into its shaft,
Goodbye shifts of grimy graft.
The miners all have lost their toil,
To North Sea gas and offshore oil.

The last boots clatter up the hill,
The last doors close, the street is still.
The coal is buried in the soil,
By North Sea gas and offshore oil.

The pithead baths have sluiced their last,
No shouting voices from the past.
No anthracite the lungs to spoil,
Just North Sea gas and offshore oil.

The factories on small estates,
At eight o'clock throw wide their gates.
And waste from lathes is made to coil,
By North Sea gas and offshore oil.

The fine edged tools in collier hands,
Fashion plastic teapot stands,
Whilst breaktime, canteen, kettles boil,
On North Sea gas and offshore oil.

Their pride is gone, but who can name,
The abstracts labelled with their shame.
And dreams of yesterday recoil,
From North Sea gas and offshore oil.

No more the shifts that changed about,
The clean ones in, the black ones out.
The miners all have lost their toil,
To North Sea gas and offshore oil.

WHERE SEVEN ARCHES RISE

I can't go again to Pontsarn on the train,
For the railway is many years dead.
The steel rails have gone that the trains ran upon,
As the years and the memories fled.
But always it seems, at the heart of my dreams,
Stands that viaduct over the Taff,
Where seven arches rise to bring tears to my eyes,
For the joys that I no longer have.

Life's flame swiftly burns as my childhood returns,
Consuming the years I've amassed;
And the blaze of my thoughts is a beacon of sorts,
That guides me back into the past.
When engines on rails, ran from Merthyr through Wales,
To places now hidden from me,
For buses can't run where once iron wheels spun
From the green Brecon hills to the sea.

Today there are weeds from the wind driven seeds,
Where Heolgerrig Halt kissed the hill.
With ghosts of the folk who stood there and joked,
(Perhaps they are laughing there still).
But you can't run on smiles down the long haunted miles,
You need steam from Welsh anthracite coal;
And pistons to drive as a train comes alive
On wheels that are ready to roll.

There's a tug at the heart as my world falls apart,
With the thought that I'll never more see,
The fourteen arch span of that poem by man,
Where Cefn was heaven to me.
My vision still fills with the Cilsanws hills
And the brook in the valley below,
While the feel and the taste of the steam on my face,
Stays with me wherever I go.

Now trains only run from the old Platform One,
For Merthyr has lost miles of track.

The engines don't swerve on that Great Western curve,
Through time there is no turning back.
And Dowlais and Pant where the grade used to slant,
To stations that won't rise again.
Re-echo no more, to a slammed carriage door,
Or the roar of an oncoming train.

I'll not ride the rails to Pontsarn or through Wales,
For they'll never re-open the line.
The boilers are smashed and they've heaped all the ash
On the once golden dream that was mine.
But Sunday School treats with their memories so sweet,
That were held on the meadow above,
Will be savoured by me, in the days yet to be,
For these were all banquets of love!

~ ~ ~ ~ ~ ~ ~

WRESTLING NEVER WAS SUCH FUN

Fingers flying over the keyboard, busily my dear wife types.
Always cheerful, always smiling, sees mistakes but never gripes.
Swift corrects my faulty spelling, punctuates my flowing verse,
Sees the pitfalls that beset me, heads me off from doing worse.

It is not a good typewriter, age and wear have brought it low.
No-one but my wife can use it, only she can make it go.
It is quite an epic struggle, wresting never was such fun.
Just three falls and two submissions and she has the contest won.

She looks in the Dictionary seeking ways to spell my words.
Finds they are my own invention, points this out but never hurts.
Brings me down from that high plateau where my dreams have flown me to;
What a woman, what a landing, what great magic love can do.

Sometimes, wrapped in contemplation, motionless she sits and stares.
Shocked no doubt by what I've written springing on her unawares.
Mesmerised by blots and doodles, alterations, crossings out,
Do I phone and tell her mother, shall I call the doctor out?

Not to worry, she recovers, starts again and steams ahead.
Tells a joke to her reflection, laughs out loud at what she's said.
Sings three bars from some old ballad, out of tune and well off key.
Turns her head from what she's doing, curves her lips and smiles at me.

Fingers slowing on the keyboard, it's quite clear the end draws nigh.
In her weakness as a woman, on the page she drops a sigh.
Finishing the final stanza she springs up from where she sits,
Overturns the old typewriter which quite calmly falls to bits.

Now I have to write my poems in a hand that's hard to read.
Whilst my wife freed from her bondage, leaves me in my hour of need.
I will buy a new typewriter, built to last and smooth as silk.
Then give up with gay abandon every smudge and blot of ink!

~ ~ ~ ~ ~ ~ ~

GENESIS

Out of a muddle of dreams I came,
Clear in nothing, so nothingness found.
All my fathomless longings the same
And every limb of my striving bound.
Upwards from deeps in that bottomless sea,
Looking for light but looking in vain,
Seeking the jelly of life that was me,
The seed of man on its journey to pain.
Nightmare shapes of unthinkable source
Swam in hells of power unguessed,
While terrible fields of gravitational force
Down on my delicate frailness pressed.
Out on the wakening crucible earth
Hydrogen flared and molecules split,
Mountains and hills to valleys gave birth
And lava flowed into crack and pit.
Moved by a will that was never my own,
Oozing to shores that bubbled and boiled,
I crawled into emptiness under a stone,
Bathed in excrescence of Genesis oil.

Here in the womb of beginning I sprawled,
Awaiting gestation conceived in the slime;
As mammal genes to my foetus crawled
From their spawning ground on the sands of time.

Yet there for ever and ever I lay,
For while I slumbered, the Giver of life,
Making his Eden just over the way,
Was taking from Adam the rib that is wife.
And the shellshocked seed of the sea spawned man,
Festering away on a sterilised shore,
Turned from the course evolution began
And grew in God's image, no more, No More!

~ ~ ~ ~ ~ ~ ~

I LEANED TO THE LEFT

I leaned to the left, when I was a lad,
For ours was a socialist town.
A valley of pain was all that we had,
With a Norman crypt for a crown.
A sluggish black river with sorrow crept,
Like sickness through channels of blood,
And there, where the fishless putrescence wept,
Our hopes oozed away in the mud.

I marched with the men, when I was a boy,
My drum had the very same beat.
Theirs were real, and mine was a toy,
But it rattled in time with their feet.
With banners aloft we toiled up the hill,
To the matchless peace of the park,
Where the fires of speech, as golden sparks will,
Illumined the gathering dark.

I moved with the times, when I was a youth,
Yet the times were a fever in me.
I could see what was wrong, with the eye of truth,
But not what the answer should be.

The dole queues were long, and tempers were short,
And men were still singing for bread,
The fathers and sons of the men who had fought
For the right to be better than dead.

I wept with the river, when I was young,
I wept for the waste and the grief.
I wept for the man with dust in his lung,
And the stains on his handkerchief.
For cups of bitterness, drained to their dregs,
For women with hollowed-out cheeks.
For children who walked on rickety legs
Through the days and the hungry weeks.

I lean to the left now that I am old,
Though the party I loved has changed.
The passion has gone and the fires are cold,
And the programme has been rearranged.
But the boy that I was remembers full well
That there lived in his dream of the past
The spirit of Man, that will always dwell
For as long as the true values last.

~ ~ ~ ~ ~ ~ ~

TEARS SHED IN SILENCE

Lovingly held in the arms of our daughter,
A doll that could speak which we parents had bought her.
They looked at each other, this doll and this child
And strange though it seems the both of them smiled.

They shared happy years for the child was the mother,
One plastic formed but of magic the other.
The doll seemed to hear all our daughter would say,
As they merged into one in the heart of the day.

Our daughter fell ill, and as she lay sleeping
I looked at her doll and I'll swear it was weeping.
The long silken lashes and eyes made of glass
Were glistening like tendrils of dew in the grass.

The tears seemed to dry as our daughter recovered,
The sharing resumed and the doll again mothered.
They played happy games and our child seemed content,
To carry her playmate wherever she went.

Our daughter grew tall for womanhood ripens,
Mysteries fade as sweet reason enlightens.
She no longer played with her small, talking friend,
For innocence withers and childhood must end.

The doll was put by (yes I did it myself)
In the cavernous depths of a wardrobe's top shelf.
Hidden by books that our daughter outgrew
In a child's headlong quest for the things that are new.

Our child fell in love, for time will not tarry,
Life seems so short and lovers must marry.
The door of her room bears her name on it still,
For she lives in our hearts as such loveliness will.

It isn't a doll that our daughter now nurses,
When childhood's withdrawn, the Lord reimburses.
And Kathryn, her baby, looks up at her now
As only a treasured young infant knows how.

And what of that doll in our wardrobe's dark corner,
Does time hide her presence, does memory scorn her?
Are tears shed in silence behind dusty books.
On lonely back shelves where the eye never looks?

Perhaps our granddaughter will one day discover
The crumpled, still, form of the doll of her mother,
And tenderly taking it down from above,
Will share like her mother the warmth of its love.

The span of our lives is a stream swiftly flowing,
We need to be loved in the Spring of our growing.
Then we too can look past the clutter and grime,
And take down our dreams from the wardrobe of time!

~ ~ ~ ~ ~ ~ ~

THE TRIANGULAR DOG

Although I'd just seen it, I couldn't believe it,
A dog with three legs that was crossing the street.
I threw it a stick and it rushed to retrieve it,
On three spindly legs and on three muddy feet.
It wasn't lopsided or awkward of movement,
It ran with the grace of a four legged hound,
And though this sounds crazy there'd be no improvement
With one extra leg to help it run round.

I hadn't been drinking, in fact I was sober.
I never wear glasses to help me to see;
And though I expected the dog to keel over,
I prayed in my heart that this never would be.
But how in the world with a hind-leg too little,
Could such a big dog keep its balance so well,
When I with one leg would go down like a skittle,
Without strong support if the other one fell.

I told my dear wife and she laughed without stopping
To think I'd make up such a very tall tale.
Then stood on one leg as she parodied hopping,
And howled like a pup that had trod on a nail.
But then through the window she saw the dog running,
As if its lost leg was still firmly in place,
And she fell to the floor, her body convulsing,
A mad look of horror writ large on her face.

Triangular dogs make the delicate suffer,
Then frighten the elderly into demise,
And though there is hope that my wife will recover,
I don't like the look that I've seen in her eyes.
On all of our windows I've had to put shutters,
With double doors bolted and buttressed within,
But if she hears scratching, she whimpers and mutters,
Convinced that the dog is about to come in.

A dog should have legs on all of its corners,
Four to a set, just as nature arranged.
If this isn't possible, someone should warn us,
So weak-minded women won't end up deranged.
I don't want you thinking I've sworn a vendetta
Against that lame doggy for scaring my spouse,
But if its got sense then that tripehound had better
Not come triple legged inside of my house!

BICYCLE SUMMERS

Now from the vaults of time I remember,
Bicycle summers from May to September.
Wimberry mountains encompassing me,
Granite chipped roads that dropped to the sea.

The click of ballbearings greased in their hubs,
The chafe of the saddle where tender flesh rubs.
Mind searing images burned on the eye,
Gaunt pit-top wheels etched black on the sky.

Pentrebach, Troedyrhiw, streets roofed with slate,
Aberfan shadowed by slagheaps that wait.
Quakers Yard Station, high level and low,
And Pontypridd waiting in valley below.

Victorian viaducts high overhead,
Poems in stone by people long dead.
Engines like toys enveloped in steam,
Appearing from nowhere as if in a dream.

Small tufts of wool left by sheep on the gorse,
The wave of a hand from a man on a horse.
A dogs frenzied bark as it snapped at my heels,
Saved by a flick of a wrist from my wheels.

Signposts that loomed from the shade of a tree,
Bearing strange names that were magic to me.
Milestones that leapt from the nettlechoked grass,
That measured a boy on his bike as he passed.

Dreaming away, my mind firmly closed,
Suddenly swerving from cars on the road.
Kaleidoscope glimpses of people inside,
Out like myself for a summer's day ride.

The feeling that here in this country of mine,
Time knew no passage and life no design.
Where all that was past and all days to be,
Were part of the heritage Wales gave to me.

Whitewashed old cottages warming their walls,
Women on doorsteps with babies in shawls.
Archways of roses on trellises hung,
The murmur of voices in my mother tongue.

The asking for milk as I knocked on the door,
The glass quickly drained and the offer of more.
Caerphilly cheese sliced on crusty new bread;
No curses or threats but welcome instead.

The knowledge that people existed who cared,
Thicker than water the blood that was shared.
More than a feeling that flesh couldn't feel,
But tangible strong like fine tempered steel.

Passing a road that the Romans once made,
Great slabs of stone that were centuries laid.
Quarried from mountains predating the flood,
By flesh callous handled and purchased in blood.

I felt I was joined in an unbroken line,
To men who had fought for the Wales that was mine.
To warrior and poet, princeling and serf,
Who came from the land and returned to the earth.

A singing of blood that fired the brain,
A feeling of kinship, a sharing of pain.
The taking of strength from the hand of a friend,
And bicycle summers that never could end.

None could command and no wealth could buy,
What my senses felt or what pleased my eye.
Coming from nothing my bike set me free,
To give my dear country dominion o'er me.

Who can forget the slow burn of youth,
Rides through the years to the fountains of truth.
Downhill to sea or soaring on wings,
To peaks in the mind where the nightingale sings.

Freedom to sever the chains of a town,
Exchanging the rags of my life for a crown.
King for a day in a fairytale land,
My sceptre and orb, the bike in my hands.

Wishing for nothing but finding fulfilled,
All of the dreams that my memory willed.
All of the longings that come to a boy,
Moving through mist to the sunshine of joy.

And always the singing of wheels that spun,
The flashing of spokes reflecting the sun.
If I could go back where my world was fair,
Then only that bike could carry me there.

With well loved friends who travelled with me,
Through endless valleys to shimmering sea.
Whose boisterous laughter, echoing words,
Brought instant flight to the startled birds.

Breath at a premium, squeezed from the lung,
Nerve endings quivering, parched throat and tongue.
How it comes back to me, now as I write,
Bitter-sweet dreamings of endless delight.

Turning some corner the very first time,
Expecting to witness a vision sublime.
Or breasting a hill with my very last gasp,
And finding the keys to the world in my grasp.

Charabancs shaking with some inner mirth,
Sunday School outings from Chapel and Church.
Singing their hearts out as valley folk must,
And me on my bike left behind in their dust.

Sweat sodden singlet and scuff collared shirt,
Short schoolboy trousers and bike coloured dirt.
Leg muscles aching and blood all afire,
Strange what the soul of a boy will desire.

And there at the foot of the hill was the sea,
With all Barry Island a playground for me.
Magical hours with sea, sand and sun,
The long trek back home when I paid for my fun.

Now in life's Autumn will I remember,
Bicycle Summers that stretched through September.
Wimberry mountains encompassing me,
Freewheeling through time down the hill to the sea.

HOW CAN YOU TELL?

Parents are blessed by their children and love every child all their days,
They see no difference between them, a feeling that time can't erase.
But as your boy child grows older and enters the world of his teens,
You feel you can hold him no longer, for manhood approaches it seems.
It's now that a gulf grows between you, and helpless you watch and you wait,
Hoping that understanding is reached, before it becomes too late.
He sees you kissing his sister, and walking along hand in hand,
But how can you tell your son of your love in language that he'll understand?
She comes in from school and you hug her, and rub your rough cheek against hers,
But what can you say to a boy who's a man, except the first thing that occurs?
Like "Good morning son" or "Good afternoon", or "How are you doing at school?",
And the words are so far from the love in your heart, you feel you sound
like a fool.
You know all the problems that face him, remembering your own tender youth
He sees you trying to compromise, for you know there are all shades of truth.
But his is a world that's unyielding, you don't bend to the first wind that blows,
And there in that world, a friend is a friend, and to hell with the ones that are foes.
You share in his own private sadness, but this you can't show him at all,
You look when you think he won't notice and hope that his troubles are small.
You watch for his smile and you're happy, he laughs and you know he's alright,
And all of a sudden the house is a home and your lives are enriched by delight.
A son is a boy who's a man before time, and a son is the mirror of you,
The mistakes that he makes are his own mistakes, but you know that you once
made them too.
You know you should show him where he goes wrong, but you don't know if your
ways are right.
You ask where he is when you come home from work, for you worry when
he's out of sight.
His progress at school you're concerned about, his problems are your
problems too,
But when he comes top of class or exam, you are proud of all he can do.
He's no good at ball games, his balance is wrong, he'll never play rugby
for Wales,
He likes to play cricket, but liking is all, for he runs like a relay of snails.
His hair is too long though he thinks it's too short and he hates every barber
at sight.
He loves certain records and there in his room he plays them far into the night.
His musical taste is a far cry from yours, but who is to say that it's wrong
And now and again as you listen downstairs you are moved by the
words of a song.
For this is his world and these are his words and the music forms shapes
in his mind.
And he is alive in a dream of his own where he leaves we poor mortals behind.

Enraptured, uplifted, he blends with the beat and is borne on the river of time,
Out to a sea in a world for the young where there are no mountains to climb.
And you hope that his ship will reach safety with the helm in a firm steady hand
That his course will be truly charted, and his future wisely planned.
No! You can't tell your son that you love him, but it's there to be read in your eyes
And if he can't guess at the way that you feel, then all of the rest is lies.
Your soul longs to search and surround him, your heart aches to share all he feels,
Yet somehow you know that he's gone beyond reach, a sickness that time
                                                                    never heals.
You treasure each word that he gives you, you walk in the shadow he leaves
And hope beyond hope he'll look in your eyes and is warmed by the love
                                                                    that he sees.
One day he too will have children, it's then that he'll have to confess
That part of his life was a desert because of the feelings no words can express.
But now at the birth of his manhood, you kneel in the darkness and pray
That deep in his mind where truth must prevail, he'll know all you wanted to say.

~ ~ ~ ~ ~ ~ ~

BITTER HARVEST

It was a virgin field of wire strung hops,
That gently undulated in the breeze.
Cloaked in a veil of sparkling crystal drops,
And orchard flanked by cider apple trees.

The fat green hops were bunched on twisted bines,
That rose like jungle creepers from the clay;
To hang exalted in their long straight lines,
A peasant people's off'ring to the day.

A billion insects gathered here to die,
As mandibles fretworked the aching green.
To briefly mate, then on earth's carpet lie
- And having passed, boot buried, rot unseen.

Here stand the cribs of canvas stretched on poles,
Untouched as yet by tender petalled hops,
That drooping hang like disembodied souls
From bine fed sprays on festooned wire tops.

This is the day the bushel basket feeds
The hessian sacks that hop wains votive cart,
While in the grass like unsubstantial weeds,
The pickers wait expectant for a start.

Now cuts the knife through base of fibrous plant,
Cascading hop clad branches in the cribs,
And stooping shoulders downward slant
The undernourished flesh from tinny ribs.

The brewers flower speeding to its glass,
Spins fast like humming top from busy hand
That later on this day will tankard pass,
To be refilled hop spiced by this same land.

So now the virgin field is gently raped,
And pregnant cribs deliver from their wombs
Potential bitter spirits canvas draped,
That go kiln dried to barrelled catacombs.

Like skeletons on gibbets dance the fronds
Macabre twirling in the evening breeze.
Hung by the harvest moon in mirrored ponds,
And orchard flanked by cider apple trees.

~ ~ ~ ~ ~ ~ ~

THE CHILDREN OF ABERFAN

The valley grieves, the whole world mourns
The tender dead of Aberfan.
The flowered cross, the tortured groans,
The names of children on the stones,
Tears at the heart of every man.

This was a place where people shared,
The bright clean homes where parents cared;
These were the loved ones, O! so very dear.
The golden yesterdays have gone
But while the heartache lingers on
We'll never dream old dreams without a tear.

We think of those we used to meet
And though our thoughts are bittersweet
The memories are lovely just the same.
The melting years dissolve to dust
And take with them the ones we trust
But we remember them by more than name.

The lovely ones are with us yet
For how can heart and mind forget
Their innocence that made the spirit whole.
We hear them sing their favourite hymns,
Young voices fade, the school-house dims
And absent footsteps sound within our soul.
Not gone, not yet, nor while life lasts
The glowing loved ones never pass
But shine like beacons in the darkest night.
The black scarred hills still feel their tread,
To blend the living with the dead,
For we are one within our Saviour's sight.
We sorrow for what might have been,
The future years unborn, unseen,
A generation lost beyond recall.
What can we say to those who grieve,
Lost to emotion, torn, bereaved,
Except that time alone will heal us all.

The once green hills that saw them pass
The battered desks within Pantglas,
Pathetic satchels flowering in the slime.
The anger in the heart of man
The flattened homes of Aberfan
The little children gone before their time.
The sadness in a father's eye,
The bitter earth where Mothers cry,
Remembered voices ringing in the brain.
The empty streets where loved ones played
The horror that the slag heap made
Comes back and back to haunt our hearts again.

Thus speaks our love through these dark hours,
Beyond the tears, the pain, the flowers.
Beyond the world who wish us well.
Beyond the words that lips can tell.
Beyond all else to that dear place
They hold within our hearts in grace,
To that embracing joy they gave,
Thus will we win beyond the grave,
Thus will we win beyond the grave!

WHERE

Where are the childhood crazes gone,
The leather thong that whipped the top?
The feet that skipped, the eyes that shone,
The yellow, powdered, fizzy, pop?

Where now the marbles in the street,
That scattered from the dusty ring?
The piping yells, the cries of "cheat!",
The canes that made our young hands sting?

The open mountainsides (now fenced)
Where we could run for happy miles,
The smell of ink when school commenced,
The shouts, the jeers, the tears, the smiles.

Where runs the Keeper of the Parks,
Who chased us from the underbrush?
Where lies his dog, whose frenzied barks,
Would desecrate the Sabbath hush?

The wooden scooters, Woolworth's sold
Two separate parts at sixpence each.
The fairground colours green and gold,
The old steam organ's strident screech.

Who walks the Market in the square,
Who buys the Argentinian meat?
Who holds the rabbits in the air,
By furry, broken, bloody, feet?

Peacocks Bazzar and cheap, bright, toys
With peas and faggots in the stalls.
The women dragging little boys,
And nursing babies in their shawls.

Where rot the apples in the shops,
Bought cheap by us as damaged fruit?
The swizzel sweets, the acid drops,
The custard creams and arrowroot?

Where are the men who used to sing,
Beneath the lamppost on the hill?
The shining tenors taking wing,
The boys' falsettos higher still?

Do stars still shine on nights like these,
Do windows open in the street?
Beats there a heart so hard to please
That cannot judge the singing sweet?

Where go the hunger marches now,
On water blistered, mangled, feet?
Past closed down pit, past rusting plough,
To distant London's Downing Street.

Cwm Rondda sung from bitter throats,
Lungs pumped with air from empty guts,
Striped flannel shirts and threadbare coats,
And shoes that leaked like water butts.

Astounded Cockneys looking on,
Bewildered pigeons startled flight.
The golden glorious voices gone,
To fade into the pre-war night.

Who brings the dark where dreams are drowned,
Who lights the night for visions born,
Who fills the moat that circles round
The tower of fear that stands forlorn?

Where are my childhood mem'ries gone
To what great store-house have they passed?
And will I childlike journey on,
Until I reach that door at last?

Where beats the heart that knew such joys,
Where fades the tapestry of time?
Where are the men who were the boys,
Where rise the hills we used to climb?

Life in its mystery never holds,
A mirror that shows true recall,
The soul reveals, the heart enfolds
And time remembered joins us all.

~ ~ ~ ~ ~ ~ ~

THE OTHER SIDE OF HEAVEN WAITS

On the laughing side of Springtime, when the sap is in the trees,
When April buds are popping and tender lovers tease.
Where meadows ache with greensward to winter deadened eyes,
Where golden beaches beckon and misty mountains rise.
Where joy is apple blossom in the orchards of the mind,
And we dream of bright tomorrows where the folk are always kind.
Where its summer round the corner and cold winter far away,
Where rivers run with promise and the roads run into May.
Where children playing childish games see Western rolling plains,
And fight Red Indians furiously whilst blood flows down the drains.
Where little girls are hopscotch bent and smudge with dusty feet
The chalked out magic squares of youth on pavings in the street.
Springtime, lovely Springtime last, the young heart waits for thee,
And distant trumpets mute my ears, for Spring is past for me.

On the burning side of Summer, where the grass is yellow brown
When it's heaven in the country and hell on earth in town.
When tents bloom in the hayfields like sheaves of yellow corn,
Where joyous throats of songbirds herald each dew misted dawn.
Where summer's sunburn's tender blush turns gracefully to tan,
And lovers while away the hours as only lovers can.
Where dogs go peacefully to sleep beneath the summer leaves,
To dream of dog days in the sun with masters they can please.
The East End troops to Margate and the West End flies to Spain,
For some the endless sunshine and for others Kentish rain,
The changing sky looks down on all, its favours to bestow,
And many reap the blessed joys that countless others sow.
Summer, burning Summer spin, a garment bright for me,
And I will wear it all my days and through eternity.

On the wistful side of Autumn, where the summer sunlight grieves,
Where trees weep by the billion and their tears are russet leaves.
There's a touch of ancient sadness, a blend of gold and grey,
A taking up and putting down, the joys of summer play.
There's a sense of something missing in the abstract of the soul,
As if the world's fragmented and our thoughts can't make it whole.
There's a whiff of incensed woodsmoke in the nostrils of the old,
And the wind that blows past Summer has its edges honed with cold.
The overcoats are lurking in their wooden wardrobe cells
To fragrantly await recall with camphorated smells.

There's a dust of frost on pavements as the Indian Summer dies,
And the sun is smiling weakly from the pale anaemic skies.
Autumn, lonely Autumn weep, no comfort can there be,
Poised as you are twixt youth and age, a trap time sets for me.

On the crying side of Christmas, when the kids go back to school,
When cold east winds are blowing and each puddle seems a pool.
When all the toys are put away in cupboards on the wall,
And rubber boots, for tiny feet, stand waiting in the hall.
Where hook-nosed black umbrellas hang and raincoats sadly droop,
Where mother waits the cold return with mugs of steaming soup.
In the crying hush of evening, when the stars burn cold and bright,
In the midnight precipice of sleep as we cry out in the night;
Our thoughts slide into morning as the icy day awakes,
And gummed up eyes, through window panes, see drifting snowy flakes.
The old stir wearily in bed, the young their covers draw,
Whilst middle age goes down the stairs and finds the morning raw.
Winter, chilling Winter pass, there is a grave for thee,
And I will bury you in Spring, before you bury me.

On the withered side of eighty, where the stairs and hills are steep,
When skin is wrinkled parchment and the hardened arteries creep.
Where spectacles poise trembling on each blotchy purple nose,
And doors that opened long ago, now echo as they close.
A feeling of nostalgia flows through nerve ends to the brain,
As all the joys of yesteryear surge through the blood again.
Old photographs, long faded now, become a time machine,
That takes the viewers back to where their golden youth had been.
Now thoughts are clouded by events imperfectly recalled,
And passions languish tepid where they once would boil and scald.
The geriatric wards are full as science lengthens life,
But age is loneliness without a husband or a wife.
So hoard with me old memories, when life was sweet and fresh,
The withered side of eighty needs its dreams of tenderness.

On the singing side of football, when your team has won the cup,
When scarves are wildly waving and you look for ale to sup.
When all the men around you are like brothers 'neath the skin,
As you boast of other trophies that your team in time can win,
There's a touch of soccer greatness in the magic of the hour,
As giants leave the sacred turf on which they showed their power.

There's a squaring of the shoulders and a flashing of the eye,
For all of you have walked with gods and drunk life's nectar dry.
There'll never be another time when you'll feel quite the same,
There'll never be in all your life such wonder in a game.
As you leave for bus or station, or you stream away in cars,
The evening shadows lengthen and the night is lit by stars.
Come with me where shouted laughter lingers in the air,
The singing side of football lasts while you have voice to spare.

On the starting side of Monday as the working week begins,
When those who stood too near the grape are shaky on their pins,
There's a sense of doom approaching, a feeling of malaise,
As if the world is running down before your sombre gaze.
Beyond the bloodshot of the eye, beyond lank hair that falls,
A jaundiced sun, through curtain lace, throws shadows on the walls.
The kitchen wears a bilious air, the shrivelled toast is dry,
And cornflakes crisp but yesterday, now give up hope and die.
Your neighbour tries to start his car, awakening dogs that howl,
As through your door you leave for work and find the morning foul.
The bus is packed and late again, its passengers look dead,
And fifty thousand hammers start to pound inside your head.
As you travel on to purgatory and pray for Friday's end,
The starting side of Monday sends you reeling round the bend!

On the sermon side of worship with the Bible reading past,
When prayer is sandwiched by great hymns and Christ has come at last
There's a searching for a need long felt, from hands that gently healed,
A lifting of the heart through joy, and ache for truth revealed.
Already words of wondrous power, extolling God on high
Have ricocheted from walls and pews and passed no listener by.
We've seen the Christ so lowly born, walk death's dark vale alone,
From Bethlehem, past Calvary, and to the heavenly throne.
No step of His along the way eludes the preacher's gaze,
Exalted are the words that pour in streams of glorious praise.
Our quality of life is raised, the harshness that we know
Becomes as nothing through the grace of Him who loves us so.
As we await the final prayer to end this Sunday night,
The sermon side of worship bathes the darkest soul in light.

On the peaceful side of battle 'neath the defoliated trees
The victors and the vanquished sit, though some are on their knees.

Some kneel to beg for mercy and some in thankful prayer,
Whilst children burned by napalm bombs get chewing gum to share.
The rivers wash away the blood but not the endless guilt,
The treaty pens scratch down the lines the enemy once built.
So peace breaks out in Asia and a million people starve,
As fresh drawn maps show some small land now neatly cut in half.
The peasant packs into his rags all that he owns in life,
To once more wander homeless with his children and his wife.
The generals and the delegates stub out their fat cigars
Then drive away from chaos in their air-conditioned cars.
Mourn with me the chances lost as now the cannons cease
The other side of Heaven waits the great eternal peace!

~ ~ ~ ~ ~ ~ ~ ~

WHEN SUNDAYS WERE CHAPEL

When Sundays were chapel and chapels were full,
When hymns were uplifting, when preachers had pull,
When out of belief mass revivals were born,
We suffered our darkness, but waited our dawn.

When week-days were speeches and men on the dole,
When work was the pit and our master was coal,
When steelworks corroded and rust stained the soul,
We lived on a mountain, but died in a hole.

When mornings were hunger and evenings were prayer,
When Band of Hope lifted us out of despair,
When bibles were opened not buried on shelves,
We recognised need and we gave of ourselves.

When choirs were singing and singing was sweet,
When out of work miners performed in the street,
When scrag end of lamb was a weekend of meat,
We tightened our belts and watched other folk eat.

When doors in our street didn't have to be knocked,
When we just turned a handle and found it unlocked,
When homes that we entered had friendship inside,
We faced life together and lived on our pride.

When glib politicians manoeuvred for votes,
When lies passed their lips and got stuck in our throats,
When promises made were like bubbles that float,
We pawned our possessions and patched up our coats.

When Spring was relief from the Winter-time's chill,
When Summer was wimberries painting the hill,
When Autumn was hopfields and tea chests of fruit,
We loved one another as seasons took root.

When Winter was death to the lungs of the weak,
When some asked for help and were damned for their cheek,
When mountains were slagheaps, and valleys were bleak,
We gathered and listened to bitter men speak.

When chapels were stages and drama was Life,
When words from the pulpit were hurled like a knife,
When paths that we followed, the crucified trod,
We Cavalry climbed to the mansions of God!

~ ~ ~ ~ ~ ~ ~

THE ROOF STILL FALLS

I'm an old man now, but I've seen the time
When fresh from school and covered in grime,
I worked as a boy with a man who was sixty-four.
Yes I know what you'll say, that it's different today,
With an eight hour day, and a much bigger pay,
But the roof still falls in the way that it's fallen before.

It's the same old dust in the same old chest,
But you won't read this in the gutter press,
By them we're painted as black as we get down the pit.
If we ask for a rise then we're rocking the boat,
We must cut the cloth to the size of our coat,
But what can we do if we find that the suit doesn't fit?

They keep closing pits and those who remain,
Still have to cope with the grief and the pain,
And the same pinched look is there on each blue scarred face.
For the axe could fall on our very own necks,
As they close all the pits in this valley next,
And nothing to do, for us, is the final disgrace.

They've opened new works for women and girls,
Turning out trash for the rest of the world,
But for men there's only a bird fouled bench in the park.
Their dignity's gone along with their pride,
Buried in dust when their colliery died,
As they sit and wait for the long return to the dark.

It's not that we're overfond of our jobs,
But there's nothing else if the pit wheel stops,
And what can we do when the whole community dies.
Do we rot away in decaying towns,
While the walls of hope come tumbling down,
Or is there a knackers' yard that the Coal Board supplies?

I'm an old man now and my butties are dead,
But one by one as they speak in my head,
Their dreams all fade and I weep for the waste of it all.
We marched and we sang to the valley's brass band,
And hailed the bright dawn of a socialist land,
Yet here we are and we still have our backs to the wall!

Our leaders have had to submit to the Board,
Leaving the colliers to carry the load,
And pay up their dues in the faded old Miners Halls.
It's the same old dust, in the same old chest,
That takes the lives of the brave and the best,
And the roof still falls, still falls,
                    Oh God! how the roof still falls!

~   ~   ~   ~   ~   ~   ~

I AM BETHEL

(Reflections on a church dying of indifference, in Georgetown, Merthyr Tydfyl)

I am Bethel, see my grief,
Hear my doors close on belief,
Watch my ruined walls cave in,
As my days of shame begin.

I was fortress for the Lord,
All His trust in me was poured.
I defended in my youth,
Priceless stores of shining truth.

I am empty, let my pews
Wear the dust of their disuse,
Let my pulpit blindly see
Man's indifference to me.

I was built by men with pride,
Strong without, unique inside.
Shaped by vision, planned with love,
Blessed by God in Heaven above.

I was Merthyr's jewelled stone,
God's unyielding earthly throne,
Made to last in every way,
Till the final judgement day.

Engines rumbled past my doors,
Trucks of coal shook walls and floors.
Molten iron's ceaseless flow,
Lit my windows with its glow.

Miners, foundrymen and boys,
Came to worship and rejoice,
Came to seek from One who died,
Joys that they had been denied.

Children sat in serried rows,
Sober dressed in Sunday clothes.
Youth that turned its face toward
The many facets of our Lord.

I was born in Merthyr's past,
Blessed by God and built to last.
Filled by prayer from souls in grace,
Shook by mighty thunderous praise.

Hymns that rolled from lusty throats,
Joyous streams of golden notes.
Poured by faith through earnest prayer,
Born of hope from man's despair.

Ministers who by their deeds,
Planted God's perennial seeds.
Harvested from Heaven's fields
Crops of love such sowing yields.

You may close my man-made doors,
Smash my windows, soil my floors.
Burn my vestments, tear them through,
God will still be watching you.

I am Bethel, I remain
Part of Christ's redeeming pain.
Bleeding lift me from my cross,
Lay me down where Calvary was.

I am Bethel, I am Wales,
I'm the cross, the crown, the nails.
I'm the bread and I'm the wine,
I'm the gift of life divine.

I am Bethel, though I fall,
I will stay, survive you all.
Still outlast the world's disdain,
Though I fall, I'll rise again.

I am Chapel, Temple, Church,
God's eternal home on earth.
Remember as my great days dim,
Men knelt here and worshipped Him.

One day soon through this my door,
Christ will walk the earth once more.
Stand in glory to receive
Those of faith who still believe.

Then will men erase my shame,
Proud proclaim my sacred name;
And with souls washed free of guilt
See my temple walls rebuilt.

I am all God's churches closed,
Father, Son and Holy Ghost.
Soul's salvation, Heaven's key,
I am Bethel - weep for me!

~ ~ ~ ~ ~ ~ ~

A WIFE IS A WOMAN WHO ONCE WAS YOUR GIRL

A wife is a woman who once was your girl,
                    and a wife is the essence of charm.
She comes to your arms with unquestioning love,
                    that stays everlastingly warm.
She stands by your side through the long troubled years,
                    as together your future you build.
Bearing your children and guiding their steps,
                    and seeing their wants are fulfilled.
Her secret is making your marriage work
                    by moving the levers of fate
Her touch soft and gentle though always quite sure
                    of the life she wants to create.
No problem defeats her, her pride is her strength,
                    who else would have courage enough
To start life anew when the setbacks are reached
                    and going becomes very rough
A wife is a corner that always stays warm,
                    a wife is a fire that glows
She makes of a house the most wonderful home,
                    in the only way that she knows.
She pours of herself from a well that is deep,
                    she gives from a store that is vast

Depleting her strength without thought of herself
                until all the needing is past.
A wife is a lover who opens to warmth
                as a flower unfolds to the day
She longs to be wanted by those whom she loves,
                for women are fashioned this way.
Sometimes she's ill, but this she will hide
                for she knows you have troubles to spare
She forces herself to be cheerful and bright
                as she carries her burden of care.
When you come home from work you are met by a smile,
                for this is her welcome to you.
She offers her lips and each time you kiss,
                the thrill and excitement are new.
You sit in your chair while she makes you a meal,
                content now to wait and relax
And thank God for all He has given to you
                without even having to ask.
A wife is a light in the dark of the night
                when your child is fretful and cries
She's comforting mother, doctor and nurse,
                who heals with the love in her eyes.
She speaks a few words as she cradles her young
                - what magic this seems to convey
Drying the tears and soothing the fears
                by changing the darkness to day.
A wife is a river no mountain can turn,
                goodness that lasts throughout life,
Joy born of caring, love from the heart,
                and peace from the borders of strife.
Unselfish of manner, unthinking of self,
                she radiates trust through the years,
Building a dream untarnished by spite
                or an unthinking action of hers.
You know she is special, but try though you might,
                you can't put in words what you feel.
But hope that affection you hide in your heart,
                your soul and your eyes will reveal
A wife is a mother who's first out of bed,
                no matter how cold is the morn,
Seeing that you and the children are fed
                and sent out in clothes that are warm.
She launders your linen, cleans up the home,
                shops where she gets the best buys,

Cooks all your meals, mends all your clothes,
                          washes the dishes and dries.
Sometimes she wonders if you're grateful for,
                          all the loving attention you're shown
And longs to be told in the tenderest way
                          that she is your lover alone.
A wife is a mistress, housekeeper and friend,
                          no money or favours could buy.
She knows what she does is beyond earthly pay
                          though the price is never too high.
She never expects outpourings of thanks
                          but is hurt by a word said in haste,
Hiding her tears until you are gone
                          and feeling in some way disgraced.
For you and your children are all that she has,
                          who else can she turn to for love
The world is your arms as she comes to be kissed
                          - for her this is more than enough;
And then in your bed as she lies close to you,
                          you look in the eyes of your wife
And pray this woman who once was your girl,
                          will be yours to the end of your life!

~ ~ ~ ~ ~ ~ ~

THE BALLAD OF MERTHYR TYDFIL

The shadow's gone, the town now lives,
Mem'ries are short and the heart forgives.
But stand with me on yesterdays hill,
And look below on Merthyr Tydfil.

Ruined steelworks and boarded up shops,
Colliery shafts with dangerous tops.
Faggots and peas in the market stalls,
Men in cloth caps, and babies in shawls.

Open top trams in dark winding streets
Well fed police, patrolling their beats.
Pitch and Toss played in every back lane,
T.B and Rickets, and wards full of pain.

Lung dust diseases, the miner's curse,
Black bowler hats to follow the hearse.
Endless processions in sunshine and rain,
Can this be all that lies after the pain.

Boys late for school lined up for the birch,
Best Sunday hats for chapel and church.
Band of hope, Tuesdays, on Wednesday, despair;
Street corner meetings for people who care.

Parish relief through a grocery cheque,
Food for the soul and the best end of neck.
The steps showing wear to the Labour Exchange,
The men showing care, but this isn't strange.

The tip called the Dandy, where spilled the hot coke,
Born in the pain of a blast furnace smoke.
My father and others with fire hardened hands
Filling their sacks where the Ariel stands.

The sinking of shafts to opencast coal,
A shilling a bag to eke out the dole.
Patches we called them, and just like a quilt,
They covered the earth with the mine-owners guilt.

Two sacks bound with rope, a two hundred weight load,
My father beneath kicking rocks from the road,
The sharp cutting edge of the coal in the bags,
Tearing the cloth of his coat into rags.

I see his face now, and my heart seems to stop.
His brow black with dust, oozing sweat drop by drop.
Trying to smile like the sun after rain,
His chest racked with spasms of asthmatic pain.

The grave where he's buried, lies high on a hill,
But the man that he was, lives on in us still.
We look at our children and through us there flows,
The love that continues where each of us goes.

My mind conjures up the back room downstairs,
The old chest of drawers, the hard wooden chairs.
The sofa all dark as if lying in state,
The brick polished fender, the black leaded grate.

The gas mantle shredding away from its wire,
My gran playing cards with her back to the fire.
Rummy and Donkey, and both kinds of Whist,
And me trying to see what she held in her fist.

But gran held her secrets like God holds the sun,
And smiled as she laid out her trumps one by one.
When she called spades, all my cards would be red,
And when she called hearts, they'd be diamonds instead.

My mam would be ironing blouses and skirts,
A pile of white collars, a mixed bag of shirts.
Her hair falling forward her flushed cheeks to meet,
Spitting on irons to test them for heat.

The room would be warm and her tasks would be long,
How could we know that her heart wasn't strong.
Her future pain hoarded in time's ready store,
With age as the reckoning nailed to the door.

The years of depression have taken their toll,
Of those who once made a living from coal,
But none are as near and dear as she,
Who loved from the heart, and watched over me.

My grandad would sit in his wooden armchair,
Smoking his pipe and rubbing his hair,
As if he would raise from the brain cells within,
The price of a pint at his favourite inn.

"Dammo!" he'd shout, if we made too much noise,
Or, "Shut your old hooter up, there is good boys!"
Or, "Fetch me a paper from Owens the News;"
And off I would run with wings on my shoes.

He died of the cancer, in terrible pain,
The suffering was long, but he didn't complain.
My gran was his right arm, and as he got worse,
She carried the burden of doctor and nurse.

Now as I write, all the old ghosts return;
Their shadows still flicker as old fires burn.
Their arms held towards us as if they would touch,
The flesh of their flesh that they cared for so much.

For time is a highway of mem'ries and dreams,
We walk with the dead and the living it seems.
It stretches for ever from out of the past,
And one human lifetime is over too fast.

And Merthyr, my town, is a stop on the way,
Those who have gone are the ones who will stay.
The living are passing, the passing is brief
And those who are left are alone with their grief.

I remember how we, as children, would push,
Our way into marches that went to the "Bush".
They'd start at the fountain and increase in length,
As various districts would add to their strength.

We took our small drums, and rattled away,
Shouting the slogans prevalent that day.
For Walhead and Labour, and later S.O.,
You won't see their likes in the streets any more.

Sometimes they promised us jelly and cakes,
Somewhere in Dowlais, but these were all fakes.
We marched through the broil and the glare of the sun,
And drifted home after, small figures of fun.

Pearson's Fresh Air fund and John Morgan's buns,
With gifts to take home for the luckier ones.
An apple, an orange, a Grimm's Fairy Tale,
If Charity's fresh, then the people are stale.

Political meetings in Thomastown Park,
Above the urinals foul smelling and dark,
Ragged we listened to each bitter word,
And went home uplifted by what we had heard.

We sat 'round our table, a family of seven,
Rabbit on Sunday was food sent from heaven.
Sage, thyme and onion, sewn up in the skin
And we on the outside, all scraping the tin.

We didn't have afters (thank God! for befores)
The gravy was thick, and it sank through our pores.
Nothing was wasted, we fried the remains,
For Sunday night supper, and abdomen pains.

We all went to Chapel, no matter who scoffed,
Except my dear father who spluttered and coughed.
Our faces were solemn, and shining from soap,
And looked to the pulpit for comfort and hope.

The good Watcyn Williams was minister then,
The love that he gave us comes to me again.
He lived as he preached, and he preached of the Life,
With his words going into our hearts like a knife.

I'll swear there were times when a light seemed to shine,
Above and around him, a radiance divine,
Making it seem that the gospels were hurled,
From the Throne of the Just, by the Light of the World.

And yet he was gentle, with heart made to share,
The burden of suffering he found everywhere.
The pain in his eyes and the love in his soul,
Were the hem of the robe that we touched to be whole.

He preached round the county from Durham to Kent,
Gathering clothes from the rich as he went;
And when he returned with fatigue as his cloak,
He gave all away with a smile and a joke.

These clothes from the wealthy would ably transform,
The cold in our bones into something so warm,
We'd feel like the highborn and give ourselves airs,
As if we were rich in our worldly affairs.

Not only these garments did our preacher bring
But books, games and toys, that were fit for a king.
They made of our Christmas a season so bright,
All hearts would be lit at the children's delight.

Sleep easy, dear Watcyn, in your early grave,
The blooms that you gathered won't wither with age.
The full grace of God like our mother's own shawl
Has warmed the long years and cradled us all.

The streets of the town were dingy and grey
Leading to nowhere we wanted to stay,
Houses on hills that the old had to climb
Taking them off to their graves before time.

A stinking old river, smelling of drains,
Means Test Inspectors without any brains,
Without any heart, without any soul,
Lord! keep us all from the begging bowl.

They speak of the dignity of the poor,
That's all that's left when poverty's sure.
For shoes to grace their children's feet,
They'd throw their dignity out in the street.

We worked for a pittance, if work could be had,
A new form of slavery, rotten and bad.
Grown men were idle, but kids leaving school
Were grist to the mill and easier to fool.

Most of the shops in that town of mine,
On Saturday nights stayed open 'till nine.
We restocked the shelves for half of the night,
With overalls grimed and faces dead white.

Eight bob a week and all you could thieve,
Slipping a Mars bar into your sleeve,
Eating the scraps of American cheese,
Licking brown sugar like honey bees.

Down in the cellar the rats ran wild,
In the empty sacks so aimlessly piled.
Making their nests where the sugar had spilled
Many's the rat that was sweetly killed.

The manager herded us all down below
No matter how nervous, we still had to go,
Tying the sacks with the vermin inside,
And hacking with spades till the squealing had died.

But what of the rats who nibbled away,
At the greatness of coal of yesterday.
Who gnawed through iron, and bit through steel,
Those rats in high places making a meal.

Vermin are vermin, whatever their form,
Whether they're human or animal born.
Though this must be said for the animal kind
They do what they must just as nature designed.

The ones without tails (or conscience it seems)
Bit through the substance and left only dreams.
Left only ruins of steelworks and mines,
Whilst they ate dinners of pheasant and wines.

Many a castle is built in the air,
Many a mansion is built on despair.
The higher man rises through methods like these
The lower his soul in a wasting disease.

Thank you dear Lord for making me glad,
To see what is good by knowing the bad.
For living with people, unsung, without fame,
Who more than make up for the vermin's shame.

Yes, the shadow is gone from Merthyr Tydfil,
The slums are replaced by homes on the hill.
The bodies of men may crumble to dust,
But the spirit of Man, rekindles their trust.

~ ~ ~ ~ ~ ~ ~

ASK "WHY?" OF GOD

Around me fast, the black net falls,
As one by one the stars go out.
Through dying eyes I see the walls
Of darkness rise to death's redoubt.
On time's sharp point my balance slips,
And there my empty shell shall spin,
As shouted questions from my lips,
Ask "Why?" of God, this grave I'm in.

I served the flag that proud unfurled
From palace roof and barrack square.
I marched and flew, and saw the world,
From ships that sailed to everywhere.
My skin was yellow, white, and brown,
But falling like the monsoon rain,
Past earth's sweet bosom tumbling down,
The crimson flood of blood again.

In some high place the clean ones sit,
In rooms bright hung with front line maps,
To dine and talk with polished wit,
Whilst brushing crumbs from napkined laps.
Their fires of rank on shoulders blaze,
On khaki cloth brown leather shines,
And through the sweet tobacco haze,
The toasts are drunk in vintage wines.

My brother weeps in muddy fields,
His body crucified on wire.
The cruel barbs the black earth yields,
Hold fast to him as cannons fire.
Around him rots what country grew,
The rich strong crop of priceless flesh,
And death's dark reapers cut anew,
As sickles slice through tenderness.

Beyond that line, the deep trench runs,
And him they call my enemy,
Lies deep in shock behind the guns,
That try to bring an end to me.
In liquid fire his bowels drown
As some sharp signal from above,
Now lifts him up, then thrusts him down,
Beyond the reach of joy and love.

The poppies raise their heads of blood,
And through black eyes watch shellshocked trees.
While sweet dead flesh sinks deep in mud,
To taint the fresh God driven breeze.
In countless homes through tortured lands,
Bad news is read by grieving eyes,
And heaps of crumbled telegrams,
Become a hill of monstrous size.

Steel helmets slant on dead mens' guns,
As monuments to mankind's loss;
Whilst fields of unremembered ones,
Are shadowed by the greater cross.

The Devil stamps his cloven hoof,
As drunk with power and senseless rage,
He tries to burn the book of truth,
That breathes God's love on every page.

Soon, peasant boots, will idly kick,
Some beak picked skull from furrowed earth,
And rooting dog will gruesome lick,
Poor piles of bones that shook with mirth.
Around the world on beds of pain,
Into this life the babes are led;
And there, unseen, the mark of Cain,
Is branded deep on every head.

From bamboo huts, from graceful halls,
From terraced slum and tenement;
From native kraal with mud baked walls,
From governed and from government;
From homes of man the ceaseless flow,
Some chilled by fear, some brightly brave,
Will fighting, killing, onward go
To some far, vast, eternal grave.

Around me fast the black net clings,
As one by one the stars burn out.
To dying eyes the darkness brings
No answer to the endless doubt.
On time's sharp point my balance slips,
And there my empty shell shall spin,
As shouted questions from my lips
Ask "Why?" of God this grave I'm in.

DOUBLE DUTCH
OR DOUBLE DIAMOND

In the middle of my garden, underneath an apple tree
I have grown an alien flower that is twice as tall as me.
I have rooted it in compost, I have fertilised it well
And it regards me balefully as far as I can tell.

I have watched it in the morning, afternoon and in the night
Even taped it with a measure just to gauge its width and height.
Talked to it in fluent Welsh at which it seemed to sneer
And nourished it with loving care and Double Diamond beer.

I've heard it hiccup once or twice and though this seems insane
I'll swear I've seen it stagger just to dodge the falling rain.
I don't believe it's too far gone or alcoholic yet,
Though it will scream blue murder if it gets its petals wet.

The other day, just for a lark, I chopped away one root,
And like a flash it grabbed one leg and tossed away my boot.
It chewed my toes, then bit my nails and nibbled at my sole,
Then dragged me where its root had been and pulled me down the hole.

I don't quite know how I survived, it was quite dark down there,
And by this time, as well as foot, it had me by the hair.
I passed two worms, whom I could see, had pity in their eyes,
As they observed my painful plight and heard my fearful cries.

I must have travelled up the stem right to its frightful heart
For I could see the apple tree as pith I tore apart.
And pollen dust flew up my nose which caused a giant sneeze
As bumble bees shot in their stings and kicked me with their knees.

With one boot on and one boot off, I felt a proper clot
For my right foot had something on, my left one hadn't got.
I felt deprived and far from home and never thought I'd see
My two digestive biscuits and my morning cup of tea.

Then to my horror and dismay, I saw my wife approach
And pour a can of good strong ale right down the creature's throat
It hiccuped twice and threw me up and footloose did I fly
For it retained my other boot though I'm past caring why.

Now I have caged the alien plant and dug a lime filled pit
So it can't choke the life from me and I can't throttle it
At opening times it pleads release and asks me for a sub
So it can join the boys and go, down to the local pub.

It breaks my heart its plight to see, it seems a proper shame,
Yet for its utter lack of beer its got itself to blame.
Withdrawal symptoms in a plant are pitiful to watch,
So now and then I spray its leaves with ginger ale and scotch.

So if you nourish plants like these, with alcohol or such
Don't speak to them in fluent Welsh but learn some double Dutch.
And stay well clear of trailing vines and never chop a root
For they will pull you down the hole and masticate your boot!

~ ~ ~ ~ ~ ~ ~

AND HIS THE PRICE

He is old and crushed, my brother,
Breathing from his only lung.
Dust and doctors took the other,
Long ago when he was young.
Fifty now, with eyes like winter,
Hair of snow and limbs of ice.
Every breath stabs like a splinter,
Yours the coal, and his the price.

Flat he lay, in muddy heading,
Swinging pickaxe at the seam.
Miners' blood from small cuts shredding,
Trailing thoughts through time's dark stream.
Arm and shoulder muscles aching,
Fine dust falling, foul, to stain.
Where this shell of man is breaking,
Yours the coal, and his the pain.

Once his voice was gold with laughter,
Mellow, warm, and sweet to hear.
Tenor tone to ring on rafter,
Or at rugby games, to cheer.
Now a thin dry wind is blowing,
Through that throat where songs were sung,
Day by day while breath is slowing,
Yours the coal, and his the lung.

See him climb the fern draped mountain,
Breath and hope are ebbing fast.
Seeking life's immortal fountain,
But for him, that dream is past.
From his eyes the light is fading,
With the joy his soul once gave.
Trapped by nightmares he's afraid in,
Yours the coal, and his the grave.

He is very old, my brother,
Like cement his only lung.
Dust and doctors took the other,
When the world was fresh and young.
Fifty now, with stooping shoulders,
Hair of snow and heart of ice.
Soon he'll go where dry flesh moulders,
Yours the coal - and his the price!

~ ~ ~ ~ ~ ~ ~

HOPING TO BE BORN

The world is old and we forget
That Christmas hasn't happened yet,
And will not happen anywhere
Until we learn to love and care.

The Wisemen haven't seen their star,
The shepherds watch their flocks afar,
And Bethlehem is just a place
That waits for man to grow in grace.

We sow the seeds of war until
There is no cross, no crown, no hill,
For God's sweet Son can have no birth
While nuclear clouds enshroud the earth.

There is no Sermon on the Mount,
Instead we hear the Geigers count,
Yet Christ's torn body must not bleed
For children born of mutant seed.

We stand before Time's awesome door,
Afraid to knock, afraid to know
If Christmas is a travesty,
Or power, glory, majesty!

We cannot turn the years aside,
Christ isn't born, Christ hasn't died.
We can but alter time to come
That Christmas happens still to some.

For Christmas isn't just a day
To drink and gorge or maybe pray,
While sentimental tears fall
Like fall-out poison from us all.

This day is hoping to be born
From truth revealed on Christmas morn;
So Heaven might open wide its gate
Where Christ and life eternal wait.

For we all shape the way we are,
The pure in heart shall see their star,
And God will give His Son to them
For they are come to Bethlehem!

~ ~ ~ ~ ~ ~ ~

A DREAM THAT'S NOT FORGOTTEN

I remember people who once lived in Albert Road,
Those shabby terraced houses down in Bow.
Who borrowed out of friendship, then paid back what they owed,
To make our cup of living overflow,
As we shared despair together then rejoiced at hope restored
In shabby terraced houses down in Bow.

We had our crumbling buildings, even houses that were shored
By buttresses of timber that were old;
And roofs with slates long missing through which the water poured,
To leak into the bedrooms down below.
But all of this we suffered for no landlord could afford
To renovate those houses down in Bow.

We gathered in our local pub when Saturdays came round,
To drink and sing the songs of long ago.
When Bert Smith on piano, his massive hands did pound
To give each faded key a mighty blow;
Then walked home all together, sharing something we had found
In shabby terraced house down in Bow.

We had our outside privies next to sheds where junk was stored,
And wireless aerial poles all in a row.
While crops of stunted flowers that were never brought indoors,
Would pollen dust on sickly bees bestow.
Yet we were not defeated and no garden was ignored,
In shabby terraced houses down in Bow.

We had our weddings where we laughed and funerals where we cried
And if our hearts were touched we let it show,
As we followed the departed, or kissed the blushing bride,
And watched the food go down and beer flow,
Whilst people who were strangers there, just marvelled at our pride,
In shabby terraced houses down in Bow.

Then wartime came and we were bombed, with many killed or maimed,
But nothing broke our spirit as you know.
We sent our children far away and those who still remained
Shook fists in their defiance of the foe;
And good old Winston came to say that he was not ashamed,
Of shabby terraced houses down in Bow.

Well, peace returned, and some dolts did, what Hitler failed to do,
By telling us our houses had to go.
While people, like statistics, were juggled by the few,
Rehoused in high rise dwellings by the score;
And neighbours who were forced apart, looked back with longing to,
Those shabby terraced houses down in Bow.

Yes I remember people down a friendly lamplit road,
A place of kindness I was proud to know.
Who showed the world a spirit that will never be restored,
Until the towering hamlets are no more.
When people needing neighbours will demand an Albert Road,
A dream that's not forgotten down in Bow!

~ ~ ~ ~ ~ ~ ~

DOWN WHERE THE RAINBOW ENDS

Dreamed I this at sunset when all the world was still,
And wreaths of interlocking clouds embraced beloved hills.
Red and golden tendrils drawn from a setting sun
Touched the mind's dark corners and lit them one by one.

As the light revealed them, the corners made a frame
Holding life's broad canvas with colours bright as flame.
From its painted landscape where loving kindness grew,
Children walked toward me with faces that I knew.

O! The joy this gave me, for these were boyhood friends,
Come to take my spirit, down where the rainbow ends.
Where hands were always gentle and words were seldom rough,
And games we played were happy for these were played with love.

Fountain springs cascaded for throats that song left dry,
Cold as ice and smooth as milk, streams no wealth could buy.
And as we drank together, our spirits swiftly soared,
For those who share life's nectar will find their faith restored.

A breeze was softly blowing and bore upon its breath
The scent of countless roses and apple blossom fresh,
And as it played around us, we children took our fill
Of nature's magic perfume on youth's immortal hill.

We garlanded each other with plaited daisy chains.
Gave answer with our singing as remembrance called our names.
Chased shadows through the hollows, found substance in a tree
And harmonised our voices with the humming of a bee.

The great eternal Artist then added with His brush
Upon that dreaming landscape, the evenings sacred hush,
And in the loveliest corner down where He signed his name
He painted that dear childhood home from whence my loving came.

And there framed in the doorway, my own dear parents stood,
Still unchanged from yesteryear when life was sweet and good.
Arms held out in welcome, O! How they drew me on,
But as they kissed my lips again the golden dream was gone.

Now I search every canvas in hope that I will find
That painted dream of sunset, by my Creator signed.
I know its hung up somewhere for it's been seen by friends
Who come to take my spirit home, down where the rainbow ends.

THROUGH ALL OF TIME

Through cottage window shone the moon,
With dove grey light on all within,
While from an upstairs attic room,
Came haunting plaint of violin.
Breathlessly I waited for,
The silent opening of the door.

Many a night I waited thus,
For bow to scrape on mellow strings.
Or moon to light the powdered dust,
That fell on gruesome, shadowed, things.
None but me that house within,
- So what dark shade played violin?

And then one night the playing ceased,
While soft on the stairs, two dragging feet,
Like some long crippled loathsome beast,
Came to my door where shadows meet.
Knowing all the Devils tricks,
I held aloft my crucifix.

Just for a moment, timbered door,
Dissolved in fear before that host.
The wood returned, but not before,
I saw that sweet and tiny ghost,
With old and mellow violin,
Tucked under soft and dimpled chin.

Two crippled limbs in leg irons lay,
Her gold hair haloed winsome face.
Through all of time I'll hear her play,
In this and every other place.
She looked with love the cross upon,
Smiled up at me, and then was gone.

Through cottage windows shines the sun,
With light of day on all within,
And I am now the lonely one
Who hears no more that violin.
Through empty days, my memory,
Brings child and music back to me.

FOR SUCH IS THE KINGDOM OF HEAVEN

MATTHEW 19, VERSES 13 & 14

I have to form words with my hands,
Just fingers eight and two small thumbs.
I hope the good Lord understands,
For I am deaf and I am dumb.

I have to learn to read by touch,
What others seek I'll never find.
I hope my Savour loves me much
For I'm a child and I am blind.

I have to live in emptiness,
Brain damaged through no fault of mine.
A light that's dimmed from birth to death,
Can my Creator make me shine?

I have to walk a crooked way,
Without support that others know.
Perhaps on resurrection day
The Lord will make my legs grow.

I have to move from place to place
Accursed and scorned where'er I roam.
My parents gone without a trace,
Will God the Father take me home?

I have to die while yet a child,
For in my veins red cells have died.
When this life ends I hope I'll find
That Heaven's gates have opened wide.

I have to starve in this dry land.
The crops have failed, there is no rain.
I may not grow to be a man,
O! Will Christ Jesus come again?

I have to stay on this machine,
That purifies the blood in me,
And trust in One who washed me clean,
With His own blood on Calvary.

I have to keep myself apart,
For those who see me try to hide.
God give me power to move their hearts,
For I was born Thalidomide.

I have to follow where Christ trod,
As only He can make me whole.
For when I am a child of God,
Then I will have a perfect soul!

ECHOED GREETINGS

Are they waiting still in sidings
All those pre-war miners' trains,
With their cream and brown paint hiding
Dark compartments fouled by stains?
Are there voices when the wind blows,
Echoed greetings living on?
Are the shadows on the windows
Ghosts of colliers long since gone?

Are the rails they stand on rusty,
Do the wheels go short of oil?
Are the wooden seats still dusty
From some deep pit's grimy toil?
As they lean against red buffers,
Silver tinged where moonlight gleams,
Are they occupied by lovers
Who would share with them their dreams?

Are the winter's dawns as freezing
As they were in days gone by?
Is the air alive with wheezing
From some gravelled lung squeezed dry?
Are the tinkers' wares now wasted,
Sandwich tins and cold tea jacks;
With their food and drink untasted
On the cobwebbed luggage racks?

Are there pungent smells from sufferers,
Rancid goose grease rubbed on chests?
Are there threads of wool from mufflers
That once wound around warm flesh.?
Are there playing cards discarded
In dark corners by the doors?
Splintered crib boards with their matches,
Gathering dust on carriage floors?

Do our tears nourish thistles
In deserted station yards?
Can we still hear piercing whistles
From resplendent railway guards?
Is there steam for wheel and piston,
Coal to feed the boiler's flames?
Are there widows who can listen
As their loved ones call their names?

Are they rotting as they slumber
All those faded miners' trains?
Or is there amongst their number
Maybe one that hope reclaims?
As it bears its load of toilers
to the coalfields of the dead,
Will it waken sleeping colliers
From the dust that forms their bed?

~ ~ ~ ~ ~ ~ ~

ELIJAH

This is a story so tender, it made even Dracula cry,
It happened one day in September as the light was beginning to die,
When a flea by the name of Elijah, a husband and father of three,
Hopped into a glassful of cider, then jumped out again upon me.

My heart grieves again as I tell it, this tale of a flea that was drunk,
For there on its breath as I smelled it, was the pong of an over ripe skunk.
It staggered about on my belly, so sozzled it hurt just to crawl
As its legs wobbled round like a jelly and its head rolled around like a ball.

Helpless I watched the beast weaving and listened appalled as it sung,
For singing demands heavy breathing and fleas only have the one lung.
It warbled high notes like a tenor with too great a liking for gin,
And the words were so wildly suggestive, I blushed to the roots of my skin!

I tried very hard to restrain it, but fleas that are drunk have no shame,
I tried with a hammer to brain it, but the flea only thought this a game.
It sidestepped the blow it saw coming, and laughed as I hit my own tum,
and carried on singing and humming though my navel was purple and numb.

It was now the carousing Elijah, the drink having gone to his head,
Began to behave like a tiger that hadn't been decently fed.
He buried his fangs in my tummy and the pain that I felt was so choice
I called for my daddy and mummy and swore at the top of my voice.

But the flea simply carried on feeding, like a cow that is chewing the cud,
Deaf to my cries and my pleading as he took his fair share of my blood.
So great was his thirst as he drank me, he grew full and round like the moon,
And not even pausing to thank me, he burst like a swollen balloon.

So over this tale hangs a shadow, bereavement unbearably sad,
For somewhere there must be a widow and three little fleas without dad.
I hope that they'll never drink cider, then hop on a bare Belly B,
Or they could end up like Elijah, who died of the drink and of me!

~ ~ ~ ~ ~ ~ ~

THE WORLD AND MY SON

Abacus fingers, computerised brain,
Mind made to reason, heart to know pain.
Nerve ends in bible, feelings in soul,
Blood cleansed on Calvary, spirit made whole.
Drowned in theology, O! what a sea,
To hold in its bosom the son born to me.

True structured triangle, sides the same length,
Angles like arrows whose bowstring is strength.
Bearded Pythagoras, head in the clouds,
Proud of demeanour, nervous of crowds.
Faith to move mountains derived from the One,
Who knows He's enthroned in the soul of my son.

Bread from the body and wine from the blood,
Grace from the saviour like rivers in flood.
Recharging his batteries from power that flows
Direct from the place where the last trump will blow
And following on in the footsteps of Christ
Communing in prayer with the Lord who is life.

Sensitive nerve ends, compassionate heart
Eyes drinking sunshine to swallow the dark.
Words poured like silver from wells that are deep,
Straight from commandments of God that he keeps.
Searching for something he knows to be there
And finding the cloak of the Gospels to wear.

Joy born of music his own feelings shape,
Song praise unfettered then helped to escape.
Instruments offering their tributes of gold,
As loving he holds them with pleasure untold.
Not to a world lost to glory plays he,
But to that Creator who's son died for me.

Abacus fingers, computerised brain,
Life based on giving but never on gain.
Humour that bubbles from generous springs,
Shorn of all malice and plucked of all stings.
Born of the spirit and worshipping One
Who died on the cross for the world and my son.

~ ~ ~ ~ ~ ~ ~

MY GRANDFATHER

There it lies, with its hopes and fears,
That town of mine in its vale of tears.
And I watch from the streets above the hill,
The past come alive as it always will.

I see myself as a child of three,
My hair being combed on my mother's knee.
Freshly bathed and my best clothes on,
With stout black shoes that brightly shone.

I feel again the comb through my hair,
And my mother's touch as she held me there.
Knowing again the kiss of her lips,
And the love that pulsed through her fingertips.

The darkness fades and that room is lit,
And I see that place where my Mam would sit,
Her warmth that blazed like the living coal,
That glows on still within my soul.

This day stands out in my memory,
For these were magical hours for me.
A time to treasure as the long days pass,
And the colours change through the mountain grass.

My Grandad waits as he waited then,
And my tears flow fast as I hold my pen.
To see him there alert and alive,
In that spring of nineteen-twenty-five.

We were going this day by an early train,
To Porthcawl to see my Father again.
To the Rest Home that lay on the sloping land,
Above the sweep of the golden sand.

It's strange how vivid the past can be,
A fragment of time from the memory.
Each side of this light the mind is dark,
Like the black of space round a starlight's spark.

A portrait I was, in yesterday's frame,
Painted by time in colours of flame.
The canvas a fragment of youthful joy,
Coming to life in the heart of a boy.

The streets I walked were a changeless grey,
But the blossomed trees were ablazed with May.
And the old Park Road in the morning's light,
Was arched by the flowers of pink and white.

The hills were massed each side of the town,
And the path through the park went sliding down,
Out to the road that led to the trains,
How bright and vivid the scene remains.

I see again every mile of the way,
From Merthyr to Swansea that golden day.
Tunnelling through the mountains that rose,
To the purple crests where the wimberry grows.

Slow moves the heart through the arch of the years,
Quick flows the blood and fast flows the tears.
Deep, deep, inside, where the joy turns to pain,
That train moves immortal through valleys again.

My Grandad eager to show me this land,
Embracing all Wales with his outstretched hand.
Taking me out through the gates of his mind,
To the windswept slopes where the rivers wind.

"There! There!", he cries, "That house on the hill,
I lodged in it once with your Uncle Will.
We worked in the pit just below Aberdare,
Before you were born, boy, I lived over there!".

Sometimes I nodded, for there in that train,
His torrent of words washed sleep through my brain.
His memories twisting like quicksilver streams,
Weaving the fibre of Wales through my dreams.

So simple his pleasures, to share there with me,
The joys that he knew at his own Mother's knee.
The hills that he climbed, the rivers he fished,
The sights that he saw, and the wishes he wished.

The old mountain fighters, whose blood flowed like wine,
With fists like great hams that were pickled in brine.
Twm Morgan, Dai Davies, and fifty long rounds,
I lived blow by blow, and his joy knew no bounds.

"Dai Davies was punch drunk, and Twm Morgan blind,
Both out on their feet with their great arms entwined.
A draw's what they called it, but all of us knew,
That the bareknuckle days of both fighters was through!"

A great little man with a heart like a child,
Drawing God's breath through lungs long defiled.
By the anthracite dust of the deep working dark,
His life was a cage, but his soul was a park.

In navy blue serge, the dress of his class,
Fond of his pipe and fond of his glass.
Asking no more of his Maker than this,
A warm loving home and the mountain wind's kiss.

A night with his friends in the "Pendarren End",
He was what he was, no need to pretend.
A spry little man with a smile on his lips,
And feet that could balance on slag mountain tips.

I shared in his home to the end of his days,
Ran errands for him and treasured his praise.
I bled with his cancer and one part of me,
Died as the coil of his soul floated free.

Men like my Grandad were trapped in an age,
When the pub was a relief and the chapel a stage.
Cold rides through the dawn to the pit at Glyn Neath,
Clay pipe kept alight in his chattering teeth.

Eight hours of hell down there in the depths,
Then back to the cage with wearying steps.
Up to the air that would blow off the hill,
He drank of its cup and he drank his fill.

But, O! the joy of the cleansing tub,
The top half first with a flannels rub,
Kneeling before a great roaring fire,
Soaking in warmth to his heart's desire.

This paid for all, and this was the life,
Hot water poured over his head by his wife.
Clean clothes to wear and baccy to chew,
And no man could tell of the joy that he knew.

I still see him walk past the brow of the hill,
To vanish from sight as the old shadows will,
Then he was here, and now he is gone,
While we and the rest of the world move on.

Through life's long dark tunnel the train chugs its way,
The mountains unchanging through night and through day.
Now shines the sun and there lights a star,
But Grandad and Wales will remain as they are.

For they are remembered wherever I go,
In all that I do and in all that I know.
No matter the lands that my footsteps have crossed,
The spirit of Cymru will never be lost.

But there lies the sea, and our journeying ends,
The moments were sweet and we shared them as friends.
My Father is waiting with love in his eyes,
And Grandad is gone as the memory dies.

So there it lies with its hopes and fears,
That town of mine in its vale of tears.
And the past comes alive as it always will,
As I watch from the street that straddles the hill.

I sometimes feel in my daytime dreams,
The valleys of Wales have blood in their streams.
Fed from the veins of the hewers of coal,
Who gave of their heart and mind and soul.

The great wheel shadows the pithead cage,
Spinning through time to the death of an age.
The old ones fade and we watch them pass,
To their resting place 'neath the mountain grass.

So Grandfather sleep where the wind blows free,
I shared your sweet world and you carried me.
Your arms stay around me wherever I go,
A part of the heart of the Wales I know.

Nothing is gone while the memory lives,
The greatest of gifts that the good Lord gives.
Grieve not, nor weep in the midst of your pain,
The love we all shared comes remembered again.

MUSIC AND MIRTH

A concert we called it, of music and mirth
    Held in the sacred inside of our Church.
An evening that started with songs sweetly sung
    And ended with bibles at spectators flung.
But now through the years let my thoughts swiftly flow
    To see my dear grandparents open the show.
As they came on the stage their hands were entwined
    Still close in spirit and still one in mind.
My Gran was contralto and all molten gold
    Grandad was silvery, fragile and old.
But O! there is lovely they sang there that night
    Grandad in navy and Granny in white.
Their voices flowed over us all in a flood
    Brought tears to eyes and warmth to the blood.
Made you feel proud they were both kin to you,
    Loyal and faithful, steadfast and true.
They looked at each other this wonderful pair
    And we who were listening were privileged to share
A courtship that lasted for fifty-five years
    The caring was his and the bearing was hers.
As they came to the last tender note of their song
    We audience sat silent, the spell was so strong.
But then like the breaking of some mighty dam
    Clapping broke out for my Grandad and Gran.
For one priceless moment we lived in their dream
    The blending of silver and gold in a stream
And all took the gift that was offered from age
    As bowing they left us and walked off the stage.

Thomas (Stone Chippings) who lived on the hill,
    Was eager and anxious and next on the bill.
His legs were so shaky he tripped on a lace,
    Lost all his balance and fell on his face.
Rolled halfway over then somehow he rose
    Blood spouting furiously out of his nose.
The old boy was shaken but give him his due
    He stood at the footlights awaiting his cue.

Hiscox the organist gave him a note
    But Thomas (Stone Chippings) with teeth down his throat
Just stood there and gurgled and twisted about,
    Buttons off coat and his shirt hanging out.
Some who were strangers, thought this was his style,
    Laughed loud and often and clapped all the while
As Thomas enraged by the callousness shown,
    Shouted for order and started to moan.
His eyes rolled like marbles, his face went bright red,
    As he tore what was left of his hair from his head.
Hairless and ga-ga and foaming at mouth
    Men in white overalls led poor Thomas out.
And even his family just had to laugh
    As the curtain descended on this the first half.

When the second half started a little bit late
    Men looked at watches, tut-tutted, irate.
As Morweena Richards came on to recite
    A verse about things that went bump in the night.
Now Morweena was deaf and she started to yell
    Forgot certain words and stuttered as well.
She looked for her cue from the prompter, Dai (Sheep)
    But he had been drinking and now was asleep.
She stared at the ceiling and glared at the floor
    Twiddled her fingers and wriggled her toes.
My Mam shouted helpful above all the din,
    "Sing hymns, Morweena, and we'll all join in."
This was quite useful, except for the fact
    That Parry (Tonpentre) got into the act;
For while we were singing the Twenty-third Psalm
    Parry was murdering "Now Keep Us From Harm".
Hiscox the organist, game to the end
    Played like a maniac "God is My Friend".
Morweena was happy for deaf as she was
    She was still singing "The Old Rugged Cross".
While all of the children enjoying the noise
    Sang loud in chorus some hymns of their choice.

Now my Uncle Tom, in the wings, to come next
　　Just hated delay and was terribly vexed.
He bore down upon her, his brow black with rage
　　And pushed poor Morweena right off the stage.
He gestured to Hiscox to give him his key
　　Then opened his lungs with this impassioned plea,
"Don't have anymore Mrs. More, please don't have anymore
　　The more you have the more you want they say, so hey
Please don't have anymore I pray".
　　Twas then that Maud Williams, the Minister's wife,
Dressed like a hambone and larger than life,
　　Got to her feet with her face deadly grim
Pointed her finger and shouted at him,
　　"The song that you're singing should never be heard
In this sacred building - it's got naughty words".
　　My Uncle was thunderstruck, stopped in his stride
And we who were family wanted to hide.
　　Then my Aunty Gwen who was hurt to the quick
Cried like a child and was violently sick.
　　In less than a minute the church was a mess
As people took sides with both, more or less.
　　Pews were upended and children were scattered,
Old men were jostled and young men were battered.
　　Prosser the Postman, his collar turned round
Was flattened by someone and lay on the ground.
　　While Williams (The Hill) the mildest of men
Was hit by flung hymn books, again and again.

My Gran and my Grandad at last saved the day
　　By going on stage and then singing away
While Hiscox the organist quick on his feet
　　Weaved through the battlers and sat on his seat.
"Comrades In Arms" was the song that they sung
　　And passions were cooled in the old and the young.
So that at the end when the curtain was dropped
　　All of the feuding and fighting had stopped.
Yet even today more than forty years on
　　This night comes remembered when all else is gone!

~ ~ ~ ~ ~ ~ ~

NOT OF THE SPIRIT

The old church was ugly, I freely admit it,
Battered of aspect, but not of the spirit.
Red brick, Victorian, angular, squat,
The old church was ugly, but I saw it not.

The pastor was youthful yet nurtured in wisdom,
Quietly turning the keys to the Kingdom.
Opening the door between heaven and earth,
The pastor was youthful, yet solid of worth.

The choir was angels with cheeky boys' faces,
The organ tumultuously thundered God's praises.
The ranks of the faithful erupted in song,
The choir was angels, but boys before long.

The prayer mats were faded and frayed at the edges,
Hymn books well thumbed on their chipped pew top ledges.
A man on a hilltop looked down from His cross,
The prayer mats were faded, but Christ never was.

The babies were fretful and christened still weeping,
Hushed by their parents and carried out sleeping.
Blessed by the water from merciful hands,
The babies were fretful, but God understands.

The sermon was simple yet quietly moving,
Founded on Gospels that never need proving,
Words made immortal by One set apart,
The sermon was simple, yet straight from the heart.

The people who listened were bonded together,
By fellowship forged in the fire of the Saviour.
Lifted to glory and cleansed of their sin,
The people who listened were heirs of the King.

No churches are ugly as seen by believers,
For glory shines through in the presence of Jesus.
Red brick, Victorian, angular, squat,
Their walls may be ugly but churches are not.

A DAUGHTER IS HAPPINESS TOUCHING YOUR SOUL

She enters your life through the door of your heart,
          a scrap of humanity born
Here through a process as ancient as time,
          that yet is as fresh as the dawn.
A few pounds of flesh and a few strands of hair,
          but O! how they seem to convey,
A vision of happiness smelling of love
          that brightens the dark of your day.
She lies in her cot, small, helpless and lost
          and hopes that her cries will be heard
So tender and trusting she pleads for your love,
          before she has said her first word.
She lifts up her hand, your finger to grasp,
          dear God! what emotion this stirs,
A prickling of tears at the back of the eyes
          as you're moved by this action of hers.
Sometimes she tumbles, learning to walk,
          bringing your heart to your throat
But you needn't worry for babies will fall
          as easily as bubbles will float.
Illnesses come just as surely as day,
          you can't guard your child from them all
But still through the long suff'ring hours of pain
          you always remain upon call.
Time passes, she grows and is ready for school,
          no magic can turn back the clock
And love twists a valve at the base of your mind
          where dreams of her babyhood flock.
It seems only yesterday when she first came,
          changing the course of your life,
To fashion a home from the walls of a house
          and join you in love to your wife.
A daughter is someone who strums a guitar
          as she struggles to get the chords right,
Or listens to records upstairs in her room,
          far into the hours of night.
You try to recapture the way that you felt
          when you too were tender and young,

But find no resemblance between what you hear
                    and the sweet haunting tunes that you sung.
It's then that you realise this is her world,
                    as yesterday's once was to you;
That everything tried for the very first time
                    is always enchantingly new.
She enters her teens, those slow awkward years
                    and suddenly you are afraid,
Seeing the signs of the woman to be
                    as dreams of her babyhood fade.
You know that the world is not made like your home,
                    you know all the dangers that hide
And fears for her innocence stab at your heart
                    as she takes the years in her stride.
You worry and wonder as parents will do if paths
                    that she takes will be straight
And almost go out of your mind as you fret,
                    those times when she stays out too late.
A daughter is happiness touching your soul
                    and a daughter is loveliness grown.
A feeling of tenderness warming your blood,
                    a memory of joys that have flown.
No one can replace her, her place is unique,
                    for who can resist all her charms,
As running she comes to be fondled and kissed
                    when you hold out your welcoming arms.
One day you will lose her, but this has to come,
                    though you can't get it out of your mind,
Hoping and trusting the husband she'll find
                    will always be loving and kind.
You can't live her life or choose whom she'll meet
                    or pick whom she'll marry one day
But there in the shadows of many a night
                    you open your heart and you pray
That this child of gladness, born of your love,
                    will pass through the whirlpool of youth,
To reach calmer waters where womanhood lies
                    on the broad flowing river of truth.
You just have to trust her to do what is right,
                    she lives by her own rigid code.
Perhaps not the same as the one that you knew
                    for the young walk a separate road.

By showing affection you make her secure,
                    by listening to troubles you form
A mind and a heart in this daughter of yours
                    that stays everlastingly warm;
And when in her room as she lies in her bed,
                    she gives you a goodnight kiss
The love that you feel can be almost too much,
                    for no joy is greater than this.
And so you will carry the essence of her into dreams
                    as you lie with your wife.
To thank God for showering on someone like you,
                    the most wonderful blessings of life!

~ ~ ~ ~ ~ ~ ~

THE TERRACED TOWNS OF WALES

Have you heard the churches closing in the terraced towns of Wales?
Have you seen the broken crosses that once bore the marks of nails?
Have you felt a presence near you as you passed each shuttered door?
Is there mildew on the pulpit, is there dry rot in the floor?

Has the faith that once sustained them taken refuge there inside;
Are there echoes of Good Fridays in the roofs where the bats now hide?
Will the death watch beetles finish what was started long ago?
Are there rats' nests in the pulpits, are there droppings on the floor?

Do the groans of old harmoniums come wheezing out at night?
Are the hymn books still in cupboards, offering boxes locked up tight?
When solid rafters sagged beneath the weight of sin they bore,
Was there substance in the pulpit for the faithful on the floor?

Are there vandals burning Christmas on the night our Lord was born;
Is the veil that hid the mysteries, by brutish people torn?
Have all the Devil's legions come to mock and not adore?
Does the Lord still guard His pulpit from the damned who stain His floor?

Is there room inside for charity where godly men once preached
Or space for love and breadth for hope that heaven might yet be reached?
As the patterned windows shatter from the missiles we ignore,
Is there broken glass in pulpits from the stones upon the floor?

Are there drunken sinners lolling in the pews that still remain;
Do they finger battered bibles while they curse the Lord again
As they foul the path to heaven with obscenities they pour?
Is there no-one in the pulpit as the wine spills on the floor?

Within these broken churches where the faithful used to pray,
Will Christian values, crucified, rise up on Easter Day?
Will stones roll back from empty tombs just as one did before,
When Christ made all His pulpits from the cross He gladly bore?

When you hear the last trump sounding in the terraced town of Wales
Will the hands stretched out to greet His flock still bear the marks of nails?
As the living church re-opens with God's welcome at the door
Will Christ grace countless pulpits as His angels cleanse the floor?

~ ~ ~ ~ ~ ~ ~

TEN MILLION WIDOWS

I have watched from ten million windows,
For the smile on his manly face.
I still hear him laugh when the wind blows
In many, full many, a place.
The bindweed strangles the red rose,
Forget-me-nots die in their bed;
For I am ten million widows
And I mourn for my soldier dead.
Ragged and wild are the hedgerows,
The strong cutting arms are no more.
The reeds grow thick where the stream flows,
His boat rots long on the shore.
My tears are the weeds that the wind sows,
My blood is the poppies bright red.
For I am ten million widows
And I mourn for my soldier dead.

I read the good book by the lamp glow
And draw on the comfort inside.
The emptiness fills as the tears flow,
To lighten where dark shadows hide.

I look to his chair by the window
And see where my heart's life has fled;
For I am ten million widows
And I mourn for my soldier dead.

I weep for the earth with the willow,
The sap of my tree drains away.
The life that is gone haunts my pillow,
To sadden the heart that was gay.
The dawn isn't gold when the cock crows,
The dreams come to dust in my head;
For I am ten million widows
And I mourn for my soldier dead.

I am left with my pain when the doors close,
As the bolts and the locks make my cage.
When only my heart and my soul knows
The loneliness spanning old age.
I watch for the dark as the sun goes
And pray as I lie in my bed,
That the world will make peace with its widows
And mourn for their soldier dead,
Yea, and mourn for their soldier dead!

A PERFECT CROSS

We searched the pet-shops near and far,
To find a vicious budgerigar,
So we could train this pet to be
A guard dog for my wife and me.

Well very soon we bought a bird,
Not small and sweet like we preferred,
But one that looked a perfect cross
Between a hawk and albatross.

It didn't seem a friendly pet,
Its eyes were evil and close set.
Its beak was sharp and jagged too,
As if it used it for Kung-Foo.

Its feet had long and raking claws
Like those you find on tigers paws
Its wings had edges hard as nails
For it had been karate trained.

No budgie cage would fit our bird
And so we took the salesman's word
To buy a kennel, six by four,
With lead lined roof and steel barred door.

This doggy house though far from small,
We placed inside our little hall,
Left door ajar (we were naive)
In case a burglar came to thieve.

Well we were safe both night and day,
No burglar called I'm glad to say.
We fed our birds on mice and bats
And juicy, plump, young pussy-cats.

Our holidays at last came round,
We knew our house was safe and sound,
For with our bird so fond of gore,
No thief would get inside the door.

That fortnight passed as good times will,
We settled up and paid our bill.
Piled all our luggage in the car,
Set off for home and budgerigar.

By now you know what we both saw,
When we stepped through our open door.
You've read the papers, watched T.V,
Seen pictures of the wife and me.

For there inside my kennelled hall,
Piled high against the stair-well wall,
With flat topped caps upon their heads,
Were several bodies torn to shreds.

Two postmen from the G.P.O.
(Tom Fothergill and Jim Defoe)
Three meter readers badly gored,
And two men from the water board.

Green feathers swirled around our feet,
Five pussy-cats, but none complete.
Eight mangled mice, twelve ripped up rats
And thirty wings from fifteen bats.

But of our bird there was no sign,
(We're glad it's gone, we never pine)
We've not gone to that pet shop yet,
To get back money on our pet.

Our case comes up on Thursday week,
Before our friendly local Beak,
And as it's clear we have no brains,
We'll both plead guilty, but insane.

Budgerigars should not be bought
To guard the home, for they are taught,
To kill at sight the men that call
To read the meters in the hall.

And as they can't differentiate
Between the folk they're taught to hate,
They'll go for any working chap
Who has to wear a flat peaked cap.

Karate training for a bird
Is dangerous and quite absurd
So take my tip, leave well alone,
And buy a dog to guard your home!

~ ~ ~ ~ ~ ~ ~

WASHTUB, SOAP AND SCRUBBING BOARD

I see her now and she is old,
The days are short, the sun is cold.
I see the hands I used to kiss,
Crippled and wrinkled and with this,
The lines that time and work have scored
With washtub, soap and scrubbing board.

She lifted cauldrons off the fire
I thought her strength would never tire
I saw her gay and I was glad
A little thought that pain would add
A little extra to the load
Of washtub, soap and scrubbing board.

I saw her young and full of charm
The days were long, the sun was warm
I saw her hands wring out the clothes
But I was young and heaven knows
I wish she could have just ignored
That washtub, soap and scrubbing board.

Her quality of life was such,
That serving all she suffered much,
As years that flowed like sluggish streams,
Were just endured as she in dreams,
Saw bright untarnished visions stored,
In washtub, soap and scrubbing board.

She poured her smiles from wells so deep
That all the tears that we would weep
Could never taint that precious flow
Or dam the joy we would know
As endlessly her love she'd hoard
In washtub, soap and scrubbing board.

With spirit burning like a flame
She lived her life and set no blame
As undermining strength and health
Without one fleeting thought of self
She worked for those whom she adored
With washtub, soap and scrubbing board.

When I recall those far off days
My heart goes out to her in praise
Though times were hard and money scarce
She bore the burden of her cares
As troubled waters darkly flowed
Through washtub, soap and scrubbing board.

No worldly wealth awaits the brave,
She saw our need and gladly gave
But we'll forever hold in trust
The priceless things she gave to us
A debt that nations can't afford
Of washtub, soap and scrubbing board.

But time and pain have failed to cope
With abstract things like joy and hope
Her hands are weak, her skin is rough
But Mother Love is strong enough
To see without regrets the road
Past washtub, soap and scrubbing board.

And we her children treasure this
The love she gave, the joy she is,
And though her face is now so lined
We wouldn't change the soul inside,
For all her faith in us was poured
In washtub, soap and scrubbing board.

Its now the fashion to deride
As sentiment what's really pride;
And if we could re-write the years,
To give with thanks what's rightly hers,
Then she would never see restored
That washtub, soap and scrubbing board.

IT USED TO BE

It used to be Dowlais that fashioned the steel,
It used to be Chapel where worshippers kneel.
It used to be dignified hewing the coal,
It used to be brimstone for saving the soul.

It used to be privileged bringing home pay,
A week of six days and a twelve hour day.
It used to be normal to bleed folk for rent,
For hovels far worse than a Bedouins tent.

It used to be right for our borough to send,
The first Labour member to Parliament.
It used to be great that Keir Hardie was ours,
There used to be ironworks where there are flowers.

It used to be usual for anthracite dust,
To settle in lungs and form a hard crust.
For blood mixed with mucus to rise in the throat,
To stain a man's life and the cloth of his coat.

It used to be funerals that rose in the street,
Followed by scores of black-booted feet.
Old bowler hats turned to green by the years,
Rough, black, serge suits with a hankie for tears.

It used to be ministers saying a prayer,
In death shadowed doorways heavy with care.
It used to be singing as black ribbons furled,
That sounded lament for the end of the world.

Where is the man who will grant them their fame,
Where is the book that will hold every name.
Where is the cry that should rise to the sky,
For the colliers who went down the pit just to die.

The trail of disasters runs like a scar,
From valley to valley and mountains afar.
Roads choked with ghosts who were fated to tramp,
Because of the marriage of coal gas and damp.

They pass through my dreams like the old phantoms will,
Hearse loads of men that we followed uphill.
Flowers of God that we mourners must plant,
Some deep in Cefn and others in Pant.

Bow your heads Welshmen and stand by their grave,
These men are your heritage, loyal and brave.
Blue scarred of face and gentle of soul,
Theirs is the blood in the veins of the coal.

Yesterday passes, tomorrow is born,
The mist lifts from mountains, revealing the dawn.
The present is with us, we live with the pain,
And make the same errors all over again.

Humans we are, and just like our race,
Prone to emotion, but not to disgrace.
Shut in our valleys, but free of our chains,
You can shackle men's arms, but never their brains.

It used to be said that we're clannish enough,
But all men are brothers, dependant on love.
When valleys run deep and the hillsides rise high,
You learn fast enough that it's everyone's sky.

Unconquered in spirit, our numbers are few,
We cling to the old, but adapt to the new.
We don't all speak Welsh, but it lives in our hearts,
The nation is one and not separate parts.

We don't ask for pity, but help we expect,
More jobs for the men whose lives have been wrecked.
Development grants for areas long dead,
We don't ask for jam, but we do ask for bread.

It used to be men who sang in the street
Some had to then, if they wanted to eat.
They tramped through the valleys, alone, or in bands,
To sing for their supper, with caps in their hands.

It used to be packing a bag and a case,
While struggling to keep a smile on your face.
Off, up to London, to give it a try,
Awkwardly kissing the family goodbye.

Hounslow and Feltham, Southall and Slough,
Money hard earned by the sweat of the brow,
Houses to rent for the labouring man,
And all their life's goods on a furniture van.

Their loss in the valleys, denuded of men,
But Welshmen remember again and again,
That home is the total, compounded of parts,
And carry their country around in their hearts.

From Wrexham to Swansea, from Newport to Rhyll,
From homes in the valley and farms on the hill.
Invisible ties link all in a whole,
Where hiraeth and hwyl become one in the soul.

We've suffered together, and go hand in hand,
We feel for each other all over this land.
Times are a changing, tomorrow unknown,
But this we are sure of, we don't walk alone.

Land of dark shadows, you'll always be mine,
The hands of my fathers' my fingers entwine.
Black brooding castles and clean upland slopes,
Hold like a vessel, my fears and my hopes.

An exile am I, but still I believe,
My breath is the wind that the mountains bequeath.
My blood is the river that flows to the sea,
My flesh is the land that is all things to me.

Tonight as I wait on the threshold of sleep,
My prayers will spring forth from a well that is deep.
People remembered, far distant, or dead,
Will walk through my heart as I lie on my bed.

We climb life's tall mountain and look down its slope,
And there lies our valley transfigured by hope.
Dispersing the shadows, our prayers fan the spark,
The upsurge of faith that comes out of the dark.

It used to be Dowlais that forged the true steel,
It still is the chapel where worshippers kneel.
Dignity lasts through the passing of coal,
And love lights the fires that burn in the soul.

~ ~ ~ ~ ~ ~ ~

THE RISEN SIDE OF EASTER

On the crowning side of Calvary, as men shout Crucify!,
When plaited thorns adorn the brow of Him about to die,
There's a touch of mob hysteria, a blindness of the mind,
A headlong rush to do to death the Saviour of mankind.
Forgotten now the hymns of praise, the gay hosannas sung,
The palm leaves waved, the shouts of joy, the walls with banners hung.
Already whips have scourged His flesh, already blood is drawn,
As that great cross that saved the world is placed on Him they scorn.
The streets of shamed Jerusalem assume a festive air,
The dusty roads are thronged with crowds who come to jeer and stare.
Now darkness gathers in the world, with pain the stage is set,
As perfect man with heavy load climbs upwards unto death.
Wait with me for God's own Son to light the shining way,
The crowning side of Calvary, shows where redemption lay.

In the living side of Jesus, where now the sword has plunged
The spotless blood that gushes forth sees mankind's sins expunged.
Throughout the land a cry is heard that to this day rings true,
"Forgive them heavenly Father, for they know not what they do!"
The sponge with vinegar is filled, the bitter gall drained dry,
As Christ prepares to give His life that we might never die.
The true believers round the cross kneel down and sadly mourn,
The light of day shades into night, the temple's veil is torn.
The final words have left His lips, the last great breath is drawn,
A man is dead upon a cross, a King of Glory born!
At last the agony is past, at last the spirit's fled,
At Jesus, sweet beloved Christ, bows down His martyred head.
Kneel with me before His cross that we might see again
The living side of Jesus pour the blood that bears no stain.

On the risen side of Easter, as the stone rolls from the grave,
When Calvary is man redeemed and Christ has come to save.
There's a joy beyond believing in the hearts of those reborn,
As He who bore our earthly sins walks through the Easter morn.
His ministry has run its term, the awful price is paid,
The tomb is but an empty shell where once the Christ was laid.

No earthly power can wall Him in, the truth can never die
The force that drives the universe has raised the Lord on high.
There's a road that runs from Bethlehem to Calvary's far hill
A path that climbs from hope reborn to love no cross can kill.
The Father waits upon His throne, His judgement to declare.
As those who come to Him through Christ, the power and glory share.
Walk with me beyond this life, the stone to roll away
The risen side of Easter brings the dawn of Christian Day.

~ ~ ~ ~ ~ ~ ~

THAT CHARABANC EXCURSION TO PORTHCAWL

On our Sunday School's last outing we lost nearly half our men,
But it's a lie to say that no-one cares,
For we often cry together as we think what happened then,
And we remember them in all our prayers.

There was bedlam and confusion as our journeying began,
Though there were worse disasters to befall.
For we lost poor Dafydd Pritchard who fell out at Aberfan,
On that charabanc excursion to Porthcawl.

By the time we got to Edwardsville, Rhys Lewis had expired,
(He should have been embalmed before we left!)
For his heart skipped like a rabbit when the charabanc backfired,
And it found a new position in his chest.

There were trolleybuses running from Cilfynydd on that day
(The Corporation should have warned them off!)
For as we entered Ponty one of these got in our way,
And we pulverised the passengers up top.

Pausing only for the inquest we changed into second gear,
(The driver must have thought it was a hearse),
For my grandad shouted "Vimto!" as he drowned in his smallbeer,
As the charabanc went smartly in reverse.

Just before we reached Treforest all the men began to sing,
(It must have been prophetic after all)
For as they reached the chorus "Take me Lord upon thy wing"
Our charabanc went charging through a wall.

John Lloyd had been Commander on a warship for a while,
And he was used to burying men at sea,
So we wrapped the male voice choir in sacks from Tate & Lyle
And dropped them in the river from a tree.

With the extra space to stretch in we survivors carried on,
For we were pleased to see our ranks had thinned,
Not knowing that the charabanc with all its brake shoes gone,
Was going down a gradient like the wind.

Now it happened that a jazzband was out practising that day,
(It was a shame for they were bravely led).
And I heard my Aunty saying as they got into our way,
"They'll never win first prizes now they're dead!"

It wasn't all disaster for of course they slowed us up
Long before we reached the bottom of the hill,
And apart from two old miners and a tardy whippet pup
I think these were the last that we did kill.

We lost our way at Radyr and we never saw Bridgend,
(Though someone said they recognised Glyn Neath)
I caught a glimpse of Brecon as we shot around a bend
But the charabanc was shaking like a leaf.

Then suddenly it darkened, though this didn't help a lot,
(At least we had some hope when we could see!)
Meg Richards had a baby and the driver had a fit,
And Idris Powell's spaniel had a flea!

Someone shouted "It's The Mumbles!" someone whimpered "Isle of Wight"
Though others thought it looked like Pentrebach.
But Mam plumped for Cyfarthfa and of course my Mam was right
For she had seen the castle in the park.

Well we waited there for daybreak and it didn't come too soon,
(We'd seen "The Mummy's Curse" and stayed awake!)
Dai Morgan saw some vampire bats cast shadows on the moon,
And werewolves started howling by the lake!

How we kept the babies quiet I am not prepared to say,
(It isn't true we tied them all to seats)
Though mothers sticking dummies in, made sure that these would stay,
By spreading gum solution on the teats.

We were found the following morning by a party sent to search,
Although they came across us just by chance,
For they'd lost their only compass by the old Cyfarthfa Church,
And their leader was a medium in a trance.

By the time we left the park behind, the Brecon Road was packed,
For all of Merthyr Town had come to cheer.
And they shouted such a welcome that the Pandy clock was cracked
Whilst even hardened drinkers shed a tear.

We were met down by Pontmorlais by the Mayor and his crew,
In front of the memorial on the prom.
And the very speech he gave us as a lonely bugle blew,
Was the same that Haig delivered on the Somme.

We'd heard the old, old, story so off we went to bed,
(It took some time as we could hardly crawl!)
And we knelt there by our bedsides saying prayers for all the dead
Who'd set off full of wonder for Porthcawl.

And if there be a moral it is this I'm sad to say,
Don't hire charabancs from Jones The Bus.
As he's sworn to kill our members since we kicked him out one day
For selling stolen hymn books back to us!

~ ~ ~ ~ ~ ~ ~

THE GREEN OF THEIR LIVES

I weep in my heart for the tender young girls,
As they walk through the green of their lives.
Passing through childhood and first love alike,
On their way to be spinsters or wives.
I grieve for the innocence soon to be lost,
Their sweetness that others betray.
For they will find rivers of tears to cross,
As they move from their dark into day.

I sing in my soul for the true-hearted girls,
As bravely their honour they bear,
Safe to that place in the curve of the years,
With husbands and children to care.

I mourn for the lonely, the trusting, the weak,
Who give what is never returned,
And pray they will find the love that they seek,
Before all their bridges are burned.

I look through the eyes of impetuous girls,
As they dance their way into our hearts.
Perfumed and powdered with shiny red lips,
And clothes that are modern and smart.
They pass like a vision of loveliness caught
In the instant of time that is youth,
And trumpets will blow as their battles are fought
'Neath the shining white banner of truth.

I capture in words all the dreaming young girls,
As I write in the book that is age.
Hopefully telling a story of love,
From the first to the very last page.
Trusting their innocence never is lost,
That no man will ever betray,
Or they will find rivers of tears to cross,
As they move from their dark into day.

~ ~ ~ ~ ~ ~ ~

'TIS NOT THE ROSE

Turn back the petals of a rose and look into the bud.
Prick not your flesh where wild thorn grows, the world is washed by blood.
Refresh its heart with morning dew, paint with the rising sun,
This is the Lord who shows to you the way His colours run.

Look to the gold of tidal shores to white carved cliffs behind.
The chalk streaked downs where seabird soars, the magic God designed.
The patchwork quilt of rain washed farms, spread on a jewelled land.
The bounteous face of nature's charms, smoothed by the Maker's hand.

Fold back the eyelids of a child and look into the soul,
Where strands of trust still undefiled twine round a core of gold.
Paint landscapes of the joy revealed, not in a drab array,
But from the brush our Saviour wields in colours of the day.

Behold the green of timeless fields, white flecked by early mist.
The hedgerows rainbow berried yield, by spiders webs pearl kissed.
The myriad coloured insect wings etched on an azure blue,
The brown thatched nest where songbird sings, for joy if not for you.

Turn back the clock of time to where the earth and air were fresh.
Before the taint of man's despair polluted mind and flesh.
When families to churches went, not seeking selfish gain
But for a voice that said repent from that dear cross of pain.

Submerge below the consciousness and look into the brain,
Take Christ to light the neural paths so truth might shine again.
Signpost each turning in the maze with words that point to Him,
Thus will we come to find His grace and free our thoughts from sin.

Retrace the road to Bethlehem and look upon the babe.
The light of Heaven shines on them whom Christ has come to save.
Look up from depths of man's discord where our torn world awaits
The second coming of our Lord through Heaven's eternal gates.

Close then the petals of God's rose, we've looked into the bud.
Our hearts are shaped by how it grows, our veins pumped by its blood,
Look to the dreams that man has spoiled, then gaze to the heavens above,
'Tis not the rose that we have soiled but God's sweet gift of love!

~ ~ ~ ~ ~ ~ ~

BUT MAGIC IS FOREVER

A pot of golden honey, and a crust of new baked bread.
A pat of farmhouse butter, or a dab of cream instead.
A cup of large dimensions filled with Orange Pekoe tea,
A spread of snowy linen with my wife across from me.
The clink of spoons on china and the rasp a breadknife makes,
The smell of childhood mixed with joy from oven roasted cakes.
The voices of my children floating inward from the lawn,
The love we've shared together since the time that they were born.
The magic that is living in a world I've made my own,
Then I am king in paradise, and golden is my throne.

A skyline stabbed by mountains, as the evening sun goes down.
The gift of sight more precious than a coronet or crown.
Necklaces of shining stars as they sparkle on night's throat,
The silver of a river as the moon trails wide its coat.
The sighing of a soft breeze as it moves the summer air,
The gurgling of a baby as it finds the world is fair.
The curving of a rainbow, spraying colour through the sky,
Fledglings falling from their nests to find that they can fly.
Joy and laughter, grief and pain, poise trembling in my heart,
To make of Earth a sacred place of which I am a part.

The holding of my grandchild as she comes to me in trust,
The softness of her lips on mine like perfumed angel dust.
The sending of a greetings card to loved ones far and near,
With words that can't convey your love, no matter how sincere.
A record spinning lazily on some old gramophone,
Welsh male choirs singing that would melt a heart of stone.
Returning to my childhood through the days that used to be;
The family home in Darren View that warmed and sheltered me.
Fragments of a million hours, a jigsaw made complete,
By interlocking hearts with souls and dreams with memories sweet.

A pot of golden honey and a crust of new baked bread,
These are just symbolic thoughts, that form within my head.
The honey is the richness that flows throughout my life,
The bread is love and comfort that I find with my sweet wife.
The cup of large dimensions fills with blessings to the brim,
And the spread of snowy linen is the robe once worn by Him.
The clink of spoons on china and the rasp a breadknife makes,
Blend blood and bone together when an angry day awakes.
But magic is forever, with foundations made of stone,
So I am king in Paradise, and golden is my throne.

A CLEVER CHAP

My dog he is a clever chap, he's twice as bright as me,
He brings my scarf, he brings my cap, then jumps upon my knee.
He puts his forelegs on my chest and though no words are said,
He puts my scarf around my neck and cap upon my head.

My bedroom slippers he removes, then using just his teeth,
He brings my oldest walking shoes and puts them on my feet.
He loves a lead around his throat, he puts it on himself
Along with that smart doggie coat he keeps upon a shelf.

With just the deftest little flick he lifts the front door latch.
Then bounding out he throws a stick for me to run and catch.
He takes me to my favourite tree, he caters for my needs,
And he will guard me happily whilst I refresh the weeds.

With other dogs he'll then pow-wow, you ought to see them frown,
As one by one with sharp bow-wow they run their masters down.
We never live up to their hopes, our habits they can't stand,
They think that we're all mucky pups, whilst they are rather grand.

I'm not allowed to interbreed, he's entered me for Crufts.
He likes no other race or creed, in fact he huffs and puffs
And carries on alarmingly if I just stop and talk
To some attractive mongrel she, out for a morning's walk.

He's traced for me a family tree that fills my heart with pride,
A faultless English pedigree on both my parents side.
He might have strayed away from truth as everyone agrees,
But this I put down to his youth and strong desire to please!

Sometimes he thinks I need a wash and eyes me up and down,
He always likes to see me posh to take him into town.
To clean me up, he throws me in the fishpond out the back,
Then rubs flea powder on my skin which turns my belly black.

He lets me take him in my Rolls, but first I have to kneel
To operate the foot controls whilst he commands the wheel.
He parks himself upon my hair, he peers through the screen,
Goes twenty times around the square then back to where he's been.

My doggy is a clever pup, so bright he seems to shine,
When I am down he picks me up, which makes me glad he's mine,
But there are times, I must confess, when I would like to kick
That ultra perfect rump of his when he throws me that stick!

MAX IS MUCH WARMER THAN BOYCE

To move the heart of the nation, to play on its feelings like strings.
　　To touch the conscience of millions and soar on emotional wings.
To never deny your birthright, to own to a land that is dear,
　　To cut through the false and the tawdry with words that are simple and clear.
To say "This is me and no other, a child of the mountains and vales,
　　The cloth of the flag of the dragon, a part of the fabric of Wales".
To give of yourself without stinting, to pour from a well that is deep,
　　To climb to the peak of achievement, ignoring the slopes that are steep.
To stand on that mountain summit, applauded, unique and adored.
　　Yet staying a man of the people and seeing their faith is restored.
To put down your roots where your friends are, to live in the place where
　　　　　　　　　　　　　　　　　　　　　　　　you're known.
　　To take your strength from a handshake, the flesh, and the blood and the bone.
To carry the hopes of a people, who see you as one of themselves,
　　Not in the guise of a jester, not with the cap and the bells.
Laughing not at you but with you, communion in mirth that is rare,
　　For we are part of your workaday world and life is a joke that we share.
To write not the trite or the worthless, to keep truth enthroned in a song.
　　Telling a story of friendship and love in music and words that belong.
Extrolling the people who matter, who dirty their hands not the soul,
　　A breed that is sterling silver, whose worth is much greater then gold.
To join in their search for an answer, a meaning to toil and to pain,
　　For dignity given to others, for pride that will always remain.
To cheer the men in red jerseys as headlong they charge for the line,
　　Recording the ebb and the flow of the game in verse that is almost sublime.
To speak of your foes without malice, to jest when your heroes have lost,
　　Inventing new phrases to make us laugh no matter how much it may cost.
To be a first name to so many, to know this is really your choice,
　　For "Mister" is foreign to Welshmen and Max is much warmer than Boyce.
But higher than all your achievements is the hill that the spirit ascends,
　　For we have all laboured together and come through the struggle as friends.
So onward and upward dear minstrel, you make every listener a king,
　　With hiraeth and hwyl as their birthright, for Wales is the song that you sing.
Don't listen to those who would change you, the dimmers of light in a star,
　　We are the people who made you and like you the way that you are.
So move the heart of this nation, give others the love that you know
　　For you are the envoy we've chosen, and we are the faces you show!

~ ~ ~ ~ ~ ~ ~

VISION FROM THE POLLUTED FUTURE

Was it only yesterday I walked green native hills,
Before advancing deserts burned them brown.
Or choreographed the ballet of the writhing daffodils
As murderously the acid rain beat down?

Was it in remembrance I saw blue skies bedaubed,
As one by one rain forest trees were felled?
Releasing carbon gasses that their leaves had once absorbed,
To fill the heavens with poisons brewed in hell.

Was it our compatriots who buried nuclear waste
Beneath these jewelled islands of our birth;
And blinkered by self interest saw history erased
As radio-active flames consumed the earth?

Was it dreams of childhood that held the scent of grass,
Or took into the dark the moon's pale light.
Or chased through sunlit meadows the butterflies that pass
Or watched the shadows dance into the night?

Was it only rumour that water once ran pure,
Before industrial toxins clogged our streams?
To turn the world's great oceans into one gigantic sewer
As man changed into nightmares all our dreams.

Was it earth's strange beauty that once made colours live,
Those perfect rainbow spectrums arching high;
And can we ever ask our Maker to forgive
The C.F.C's that wiped them from the sky?

Was it only moments gone before the polar ice,
Discharged its liquid burden in the sea?
When all the world's flood barriers could never quite suffice
To stop its waters rolling over me.

Was it children screaming that disturbed the requiem
That heralded the passing of mankind.
And did the deafening climax of that final great amen
Disintegrate creation God designed?

Will we be applauded when the final curtain falls
And earth's last grand theatre stands forlorn?
For who can call for encores from the circle or the stalls
When the drama that is living is withdrawn?

~ ~ ~ ~ ~ ~ ~

GOD IS

Isaiah Chapter 53

God is the Christ who was bruised in our stead
Crushed and then finally slain
A lifetime of loving surrendered for us,
Perfection rewarded with pain.
Oppressed and afflicted, He spoke no defence
But carried our sorrows and grief.
Pierced for transgressions He didn't commit,
Murdered for our unbelief.
Despised and rejected by those He would save,
Familiar with suffering and loss.
Bearer of scars of the whip and the nails,
And bowed by the weight of a cross.
Marked by iniquities never His own,
Ridiculed, slandered and crowned
Not by a diadem fashioned in Heaven
But plaited with thorns all around.
He towers in majesty over the world
Yet humbly He washes our feet,
Then hurries to meet us with arms opened wide
The least of His subjects to greet.
God is eternity biding its time,
The grace of the Lord Jesus Christ.
Goodness immaculate, free from all sin,
The way, the truth and the life.
Before the beginning His consciousness was,
He'll be there long after the end.
Alpha, Omega, first to the last
Our personal Saviour and friend.
And as we walk heavenward, our eyes to the stars
As sinners repentant all must
We'll come to a God we've been longing to see
And find He is waiting for us!

THE COLLIER

Each one in his turn is marked by coal,
Each one bears its burn upon the soul.
Each one as he talks his hardships tell,
Each one as he walks comes forth from hell.

Commoners and kings are one to him,
Dark that each day brings his vision dims.
Dust that clogs the lungs sets in its mould,
Changing collier young to collier old.

Politics bring light into his eyes;
Days of bitter strife have made him wise,
Proud he shakes the hand his mate extends,
Life is nothing if unshared with friends.

Danger is his bride in widow's weeds;
Death walks by his side but no-one heeds.
Gentle though his tread, the earth still shakes,
And around the dead its burial makes.

Comradeship to him is more than love,
And need is met when words are not enough.
His links are forged in blood and splintered bone,
And roads he takes are never walked alone.

Many are the targets of his wit,
For humour is his prop within the pit,
Who else would laugh where darkness reigns supreme,
Or change a living nightmare to a dream.

His children are his future and his pride,
He seeks for them what he has been denied.
He sacrifices what a father must
That they might breathe the air and not the dust.

His thirst for knowledge drives him to that brook
Where words of magic pour from every book.
He haunts the Public Libraries to find
The fulcrum that moves mountains in his mind.

Each one in his turn is marked by scars
Each one's dark unstudded by the stars.
He buys through toil what life would grudging sell,
And having bought, walks sunwards out of hell!

~ ~ ~ ~ ~ ~ ~

WELSH VALLEY, 1935

Rising from the valley's highways,
From the streets and from the squares.
From the dark forbidding byways,
From the market stalls and fairs,
Talking, singing, without ending,
Decibels beyond belief,
Like a thunder cloud ascending,
With Vesuvius underneath.
Talent contests by the dozen,
Crooners, dancers, large and small.
Uncle, aunty, father, cousin,
In each faded Miners Hall.
Shirley Temple's or Bing Crosby's,
Strangled larynx, tapping feet,
With great songs from Iolanthe
From each copper on his beat.

Oratorios in the chapels,
Voices merging into gold.
Lusty girls with cheeks like apples,
Blending with the withered old.
Cheapjacks trading in the markets
Trying vainly to out roar
Husky cries from sideshow barkers
In the fairground just next door.

Ancient tramcars always clanging,
Rattling wheels in rutted rails.
Sally Army, cymbals banging,
Brass euphoniums mournful wails.

Costermongers horses neighing,
Rag-and-Bone mens' strangled speech.
Men and boys mouth-organs playing,
Some old harpy's strident screech.

Buskers vying for each penny
Down the terraced hilly streets,
From the poor who haven't any
Decent shoes to grace their feet.
Sisters singing with their brothers
Huddled round old battered prams;
God protect these mites and others
From their callous dads and mams.

Preachers thund'ring from their pulpits,
Choirs shouting great Amens.
Boys Brigades with drums and trumpets,
Grunting pigs and cackling hens.
Steelworks hooters fiendish blaring,
Hellish whines from pithead wheels.
Tortured screams from un-oiled bearings,
Metal thuds from steel capped heels.

Jazzband marchers' competitions,
Chocolate Soldiers, Picadors.
Blowing all their inhibitions
Through kazoos without a pause.
Up to Heaven the noise is lifted,
May the Great One listening there,
Take sweet music from the gifted
For His angels all to share.

Like a stormcloud charged with thunder,
Decibels of noise collect.
Poised to blow us all asunder
If allowed to go unchecked.
If we prod it, make it vicious,
Send it one more brazen clang,
Then the world ends not in whimpers
But with one colossal bang!

SARAN

Sarah Anne, O Sarah Anne,
Called in love the sweet Saran.
Brown hair, grey, then snowy white,
Changed yet changeless in our sight.

The way she looked, the way she smiled,
Speaking Welsh to me, a child.
Fingers lacing through my hair,
She walks beside me everywhere.

I see her vanish up the street,
Best hat on and black coat neat.
Off to Church with Mam and friends,
The good fight fought as Sabbath ends.

Imperial mints from Drews the shop,
Soft inside and hard on top.
High above the intoned prayer,
The sound of sucking everywhere.

The outsides cracked as hymns began,
But not a crunch from sweet Saran;
Just golden pourings of her voice,
"Rejoice! again I say, Rejoice!"

O Lord of hosts keep her for us,
And keep her safely in your trust.
So that in heaven where Thou art King,
We'll hear that sweet contralto sing.

My Gran she was, my Gran she is,
For we are ones who knew her kiss.
No matter now that she is gone,
While in our hearts her love lives on.

She walks again in Darren View,
And I a child at play there too.
The years are gone whilst I remain,
To bring to life her love again.

The way we played those many games,
Of cards with rich and flowing names.
Strip Jack Naked, Knockout Whist,
With trumps like garlands in her fist.

Eyes through glasses perched on nose,
Now they open, now they close.
Hypnotised I'd lead a spade,
But Granny won when Granny played.

Spoof we played straight from the pack,
I'd lay a ten, she'd lay a Jack,
I'd have the Ace, she'd keep the deuce,
I tried to win, but what's the use.

Rummy played to one-o-one,
She'd get to ninety just for fun,
But when I tried to win the game,
She'd call for Rummy just the same.

I like to think she plays on yet,
Out of danger, out of debt.
Sweet mouth pursed and dewy eyed,
But shrewd and cunning deep inside.

Upstairs in bed, in that back room,
Her candle shone to light the gloom.
The magazines propped by her knees,
Disturbed by windows' draughty breeze.

Late at night with my light gone,
I'd creep to where her candle shone,
And pushing open wide her door,
Like Oliver I'd ask for more.

Drawers would open, drawers would shut,
Accompanied by Gran's tut! tut!
Then at last a stump we'd find,
A flickering wick to hide behind.

Back to bed to wait until,
The colliers bus came up the hill.
The crash of doors, the shouts of men,
The coming home of Uncle Len.

Through crack of door at Gran I'd peep,
Still sitting up, but fast asleep.
Forgotten now the time that flies,
The cares that live, the hope that dies.

I like to think she dreams on yet,
Of happy days she can't forget.
Of lonely paths on mountainsides,
With strong young men to walk besides.

Of valley winds that like a prayer,
Whispered through her flowing hair,
Of virgin streams from limestone springs,
Of yellow gorse and nettle stings.

To stand again where wildflowers are,
Before the plane or motorcar,
Before the senseless noisy rage,
Of living in this modern age.

When chapels rang with steel and gold,
Sopranos sweet and basses bold.
Contraltos mixed with sweetly sung,
Falsetto pourings from the young.

To see God's world from hillside crests,
Where wild things run and bracken rests.
And Wales as this proud land should be,
From mans' contamination, free.

Sarah Anne, Oh! Sarah Anne,
Called in love the sweet Saran,
Heart remembered long by me,
Walk time's sweet pathways endlessly.

~ ~ ~ ~ ~ ~ ~

CHOIR PRACTICE

Handel's "Messiah" we were practising for,
    As Idwal (Top Note) of the prominent jaw
Was waving his baton as time he did beat
    In Capel Bethania down Mordecai Street.
I was a tenor and seated far back,
    With five friends called Gareth and three christened Jack,
Augmenting the basses and strong baritones,
    -Six men called Williams and five who were Jones.
Two rows below them in headscarf or hat,
    Sopranos, contraltos, and my Granny sat.
Dai Morgan (caretaker) who lived on his own,
    Had Lightning, his whippet, who chewed on a bone
And whimpered and howled with the tenors and me,
    Sometimes crescendo, but always in key.
Up on its hind legs and belting away,
    Proving to all that each dog has its day.
Parry, the organist, having no choice,
    Had brought his wife Blod of the quivering voice,
Which wasn't soprano, but hollow and weak
    Just like a crow with a worm in its beak.
Now she was racing along a top A,
    Turning poor Idwal quite visibly grey
And making him dig his chin in his craw
    Bruising his chest with his prominent jaw
As he tried with his baton to make her slow down,
    Waving his arms like a broken down clown,
While we for our part just tried to catch up
    With screaming sopranos and Dai Morgan's pup
Urging us on in a wild madcap chase,
    That got us all nowhere but red in the face
The basses and baritones, not to be beat,
    Got off their backsides and rose to their feet,
As if by this movement they might get ahead,
    To ambush poor Blodwen as onward she sped.
Parry, the organist, unnerved by the scene,
    Was trapped by their voices and caught in between,
Causing his hands from the keyboard to drop

And blacking one eye on a huge organ stop.
His feet slipped from pedals, his bottom from chair,
His wig fell off sideways, revealing no hair,
While out from his mouth, his false teeth did go,
To chatter away on the wooden block floor,
And though you may think I am stupid and dense,
I'll swear it's the only time Parry made sense!
But just as he spun, his legs did a jig,
For they were as false as his teeth and his wig,
And though they were strapped to his pelvis and hips,
Cork legs won't stay if they're cracked like two whips.
So they shot through the air and knocked Idwal down,
And I noticed in passing that one shoe was brown
Which knowing poor Parry quite threw me aback,
For I could see plainly the other was black.
With nothing much left of the organist's charms,
(Excepting bald head, his trunk and his arms)
I followed with interest the plight of his pegs,
Which tangled with Idwal and grabbed at his legs.
Making his trousers unerringly fall
Revealing statistics, not vital, but small!
The women were screaming apportioning blame,
But Blodwen was cheering for she had no shame,
And sportingly rushed to be first at his side,
To use her best hat his discomfort to hide.
Unlucky for Idwal, her hatpin was there,
Making him leap like a goat in the air,
While screaming blue murder in North Walian Welsh
Which we in the South know is bad for the health.
He ran round the vestry like wild game in flight,
Opened the door and was lost in the night,
Followed by Lightning, the whippet, and Blod,
(For quite different reasons I hasten to add!)
For Lightning was hungry and wanted a snack,
While Blodwen just wanted her hat and pin back.
Inside of the vestry, with order restored,
Dai took the baton, but him we ignored,
For none of us wanted to go blithely on
With Parry in sections and poor Idwal gone.

So just like a jig-saw we put Parry back,
        And though hard at first, we soon got the knack,
Fitting the legs to the pelvis and hips,
        Pushing his teeth through the gap of his lips.
His wig was a problem, so greasy his head,
        It wouldn't stay put until Dai Morgan said,
"Hand me my chewing gum stuck to that chair,
        And I will make sure his head and his hair,
Will stay put forever, or longer perhaps,
        So hand me my bubble gum, there is good chaps".
With Parry assembled, Dai gave us the nod,
        And practice resumed without Idwal and Blod,
Who loth though I am to outright condemn,
        I can't really say that we hankered for them,
But rather missed Lightning because it was he
        Who howled halleluyiahs much louder than we,
And whimpered the solos with tears in his eyes,
        That influenced the judges to give us first prize.
So if you hear singing come sweet from a pup,
Stand for no nonsense but gather him up,
And bring him to practice on wings that are fleet,
        To Capel Bethania, down Mordecai Street!

~ ~ ~ ~ ~ ~ ~

WHEN YOUR WORLD IS ONE YEAR OLD

I see her like a beacon in the twilight of my lifetime,
As the burning of her spirit kindles flames within my soul.
And the fanning of its embers, sending sparks forever flying,
Lights a starry constellation in a galaxy of gold.

I fold her thoughts within me as she feels each new experience,
And the pattern of her thinking makes me young and clean again.
For she sees the world through colours that are so rich in appearance,
That they form an arch around her like a rainbow after rain.

I breathe each sigh she utters and I drink each sound she makes,
For the blending of such music is a rhapsody sublime;
And this music in her absence, the memory awakens,
To thrill our home with echoes that will last through all of time.

I see her like a jewel in the brilliance of her childhood,
And the glory of its setting puts this tawdry world to shame,
For she sparkles like a diamond on the throat of bright tomorrows,
In the necklace that's engraven with the wonder of her name.

I hold her in her nearness to the mainspring of my being,
And the sweetness of her springtime makes my autumn seem so fresh.
That I take flowers she gathers from the garden of my feelings,
And place them with her fragrance in the vase of tenderness.

I keep her close beside me as my mind and heart enfold her,
For the aura that surrounds her reaches me where'er I go.
While the pleasure of remembrance of her softness as I hold her,
Is a dream outside of sleeping and the greatest joy I know.

I treasure every moment that we tread this earth together,
For the offering of such beauty is a gift I can't ignore.
So I take it from her gladly, with a love that lasts forever,
And I keep it safe within me, where life's precious things are stored.

I toast her in her birthday in the wine of new beginning,
As she stumbles on the threshold, of an ever changing world.
May the streams of grace and mercy, flowing outward from God's kingdom,
Cleanse the soul and bathe the spirit of this lovely baby girl.

Written in love for Kathryn Mary's first birthday, August 18th 1986

~ ~ ~ ~ ~ ~ ~

A SINGULAR PERSON

No-one is born without shaking the earth, for who knows how each
child may grow.
Changing the course of a nation's affairs, or sinking to depths that are low.
Yet flesh born of woman is made to be loved, be it of pauper or king,
For who can resist their endearing charms, or the glory of living they bring.
Babies are treasure troves found in the heart, jewels no money can buy.
Gems beyond price are the smiles that they give, pearls are the tears they cry.
Silver and gold their very first words, diamonds the first teeth they grow,
While riches derived from their bottomless trust, stay with you wherever you go.

Babies are talcum that's powdered so fine, it settles in each tender fold,
Easing the harshness of red angry skin and bringing sweet pleasure untold.
It perfumes the flesh as it soothes away hurt, massaging and healing in one,
As baby smiles lost with the coming of pain, return like the rays of the sun.
A baby is hope that a marriage will last, uniting both husband and wife,
Flesh of their flesh that had mingled in love, producing this wonder of life.
A flower that grows in the warmth of your home, cherished and
                                                    tended by those
Who see this plant thrive in the soil that is joy, as it blossoms and blooms
                                                    like a rose.
A baby is magic without sleight of hand, happiness flowing in streams.
Fulfilment of wishes and answers to prayers, reality built on your dreams.
Trusting eyes anxiously scanning your face, seeking assurance and love,
Then holding your fingers with strength from the heart and finding
                                                    that this is enough.
A baby is part of the summit of life, a peak that we all must ascend.
The future wrapped up in cot or a shawl, a promise of life without end.
A singular person uniquely itself, whether a girl or a boy
A fusion of cells with a mixture of genes, created by one act of joy.
A baby is water splashed from a bath, tenderness scented with hope.
Silken hair spun from gossamer threads, pleasure in bubbles of soap.
Chuckles of merriment born in the soul, gurgles and cries of delight.
Arms held toward you imploring your touch as you comfort each fear
                                                    in the night.
But most of all babies are part of yourself, a small carbon copy of you.
Blood of your blood and bone of your bone, made into something that's new.
Someone you'll cherish the rest of your life, sweetness you'll nourish each day.
A life that you place at the heart of your plea as you kneel in the
                                                    darkness to pray.
And there in that hour with your baby asleep, from love that's the greatest
                                                    you've known,
You offer up thanks to a listening God, for the wonderful blessing you own!

THOSE DEAR SWEET DAYS

In those dear, sweet, days when my mam was young
I remember so well all the hymns that we sung.
And the saints and sinners we worshipped among,
In those dear, sweet ,days when my mam was young.

The pulpit, the people, the Sunday smell
Of peppermints crunched in the jaws of hell.
The sniffers of snuff, the weak and the well,
The pulpit, the people, the Sunday night smell.

The minister preached from his closeness with God
And even the old were unwilling to not,
But followed the path that our Saviour trod,
As the minister preached from his closeness with God.

I listened to speeches in Thomastown Park,
To the murmur of crowds and a dog's lonely bark.
To the bumble of bees, to the lilt of the lark,
As I listened to speeches in Thomastown Park.

I followed the drum of the Gala parade,
My mind full of dreams, my future plans made.
For how could I know that a boys dreams can fade,
As I followed the drum of the Gala parade.

In the dead of the night from the middle shift
The men came home from the pit and the drift.
And their dust scarred lungs took the nightwind's gift,
In the dead of the night from the middle shift.

The gas lamp shone and I heard a voice,
"I am the light of the world, rejoice!
Yet I was a poor man too, by choice."
And the lamps went out, but not that voice.

I blew out my candle and said a prayer
To the collier dead and the shrouds they wear,
For I felt them around me everywhere,
As I blew out my candle and said a prayer.

And there in the dark, as the footsteps died,
The past and the future so mingled inside
That I knew why we laughed and knew why we cried,
In there with the dark as the footsteps died.

The stars struck sparks from the midnight sky,
The scudding clouds made the moon's face fly.
The day had lived that the day might die,
As the stars struck sparks from the midnight sky.

In those dear sweet days when my mam was young,
Life was a fire and death was hymn sung.
And I loved all the people I wandered among,
In those dear sweet days when my mam was young.

~ ~ ~ ~ ~ ~ ~

AND NOBODY SPEAKS TO THE POPE

"I light the stars", said the seedy old man,
"Also the candles of hope.
I dress the earth with grass where I can,
And speak of God, with the Pope.
Rivers I stock with the rainbow trout,
Mountains I cover with pine.
With tides I move the waters about,
The sun and planets are mine.
I touch the moon with the flint of love,
To make this lantern a pearl.
That pendant hangs from the heavens above,
To banish the dark of the world".

The thunder rolls in the crouching hills,
The rain stings a billion cheeks.
From the seedy old man the water spills,
While the wind through the valley, shrieks.
The lightning strikes, and the old man dies,
And the stars are sparked no more.
The pendant moon unchains the tides,
And the waters touch no shore.

The planet necklace chokes the sun,
Snuffing the candles of hope,
While blades of grass die one by one,
With pine on the mountain slope.

For the earth is dead like the seedy old man,
And nobody speaks to the Pope.

THAT HILL IN ABERFAN

The grass is slow in growing on that hill in Aberfan.
And from the train the black shows through as only coal dust can.
The tip is gone but not erased from deep within the mind
And hearts are sore in Merthyr Vale where pithead wheel still winds.

There are people grieving for the time when life was good.
Children still who stand and stare where Pantglas School once stood.
A different generation but their voices sound the same
As the ones who shouted "Present"! when the teachers called their name.

The grave is kept well tended and there's flowers where children lie,
But memories aren't buried here, for these will never die.
They're kept alive within the mind and cherished in the soul,
As many thousand others are whose lives were wrecked by coal.

It isn't hard to understand the way that parents feel.
It takes a lifetime sometimes for the broken heart to heal.
The sounds of children playing in the streets or on the hill,
Are echoes of another time that comes to haunt them still.

They've built a fine new centre and a first class swimming pool,
With children learning lessons in a well equipped new school;
But some will never use them, or see the sky above,
For they are gone forever and we think of them with love.

The waste from that great ugly tip that crushed the brightest hopes,
Has gone for other uses now, far from the valley slopes.
The very roads are made of it and most were built on gain,
But folk still walk a lonelier path that only leads to pain.

The day may come when grief must fade and sorrows all grow dim,
For there are many shades of grey and life's not always grim.
But the flame that lights the spirit and the fire of love in Man,
Will never be extinguished on that hill in Aberfan!

~ ~ ~ ~ ~ ~~

ODE TO MY SISTER EDNA

Tell me something now, dear sister
As you speak my funny rhymes.
Do you get much satisfaction
As you read between the lines?
Do folk laugh whilst you're reciting,
Do folk grin at some daft word?
Can you see if they are tickled
By a couplet quite absurd?

Do their rumblings move their muscles,
Do their guffaws shake their hats?
Do they smile and twitch their nostrils,
Do they buzz like summer gnats?
Can you tell if some are sleeping,
Can you see inside their dreams?
Can you know what they are thinking
As each listener blandly beams?

Maybe they have slid off somewhere,
To some world they knew as girls.
Maybe they are chasing rainbows
As the breezes move their curls.
Running barefoot through their childhood
Mountain grasses tickling toes.
Where the green fern sprays its branches,
Where the purple wimberry grows.

Can it be that they're not with you
As you swim before their gaze.
That their minds have put up shutters,
That their eyes are double glazed.
Could it be that they're rememb'ring
Strong young men and kisses sweet,
As they nod and smile politely
From their hard and wooden seats.

I would like to think they're laughing,
Not at me but at the past.
When some funny child was clowning,
Showing off before the class.
Making fun of silly teachers,
Whilst their crumpled backs were turned.
Sticking tongues out, flicking rulers,
With life's lesson still unlearned.

It's quite easy, writing verses,
With a humorous end in view.
I just think of all our failings,
All the daft things that we do.
We're all jesters from our cradles.
Life's a comedy and farce.
There is nothing in our natures
Quite so precious as a laugh.

Keep reciting then dear sister,
I will mastermind your voice.
Maybe folk will get the message,
See the joke and then rejoice.
Laughter is the finest tonic,
Better far than drugs or pills,
Through these words that I have written,
May we cure life's greatest ills!

~ ~ ~ ~ ~ ~ ~

FEED IT ON GREEN STUFF

I went to buy cheese from my small corner shop
That was run by a grocer called Mog.
He once had been married but her he did swop
For a tortoiseshell cat and a dog.
He wasn't hygienic, he smelled like a skunk,
And the faggots he kept on his shelves,
Would stagger about as if they were drunk,
And would walk through the door by themselves.
Well he sliced me some cheese on a filthy rag mat,
With a knife that he used to cut soap.
Wrapped it in paper from under the cat
And tied it with two strands of rope.
Guessed at its weight as he rung up the cash
And I noticed as his hand touched mine
That the palm and the fingertips were smothered in rash
Of a puce impetigo design.

I'd heard from my neighbours Mog's cheese had been known
To put up a fight with the rats.
Would tackle Alsatians to grab at a bone
And frighten the life out of cats
It wasn't just animals that it would seize,
If cornered it went for the throat,
And no man who saw it would take on this cheese,
Without looking round for support.

As I left the grocers, my parcel spun round,
As it tried to escape from my hand.
But I squeezed it so tight that it uttered a sound
That was heard the whole length of the land.
It wasn't in English, Dalmatian or French
But like a rhinoceros in pain.
A cry from a cheese that was broken in health,
For a chance to start over again.

I couldn't be cruel, I knelt in the dust,
And put that poor dairy food down.
Cut off the wrappings in which it was trussed,
And showed it the way to the town.

It turned on its heels, that evil old cheese,
And then for my jugular sprang,
And offered no thanks as it nibbled my knees,
As it brought me to earth with a bang.

A cheese, if it's bad, must be put in a cage
No matter how much it may plead,
And though it may shake the bars in its rage,
It's better to pay it no heed.
Feed it on green stuff but never on bone
Give it not whisky or gin.
Or it will take over the rest of your home
And savage the people within!

~ ~ ~ ~ ~ ~ ~

IN THE VALE WHERE WE DWELL

This is the town into which I was born,
Resources exploited, its greatness in pawn.
Iron and steel on great mountains of coal,
Mourned in their passing by men on the dole.
Who stood on street corners and watched their demise
With fear in their hearts and despair in their eyes.
For no man could reason and no voice could tell,
Why hope had to die in the vale where we dwell.

I've lived my life through but to those who remain,
I leave as a legacy words born of pain.
With verses that chronicle, lines that will draw
The map of an age from the scenes that I saw.
Of those who refused to surrender their pride,
Leaders of men with great passion inside,
Who rallied and succoured the weak and the well,
In need of their strength in the vale where we dwell.

And unemployed miners who used basic skills,
To hew stolen coal from deep shafts in the hills.
Who, driven by hunger, surrendered esteem,
Down there in the filth of an opencast seam.

As flames of resistance from fires in the soul
Illumined the dark of each waterlogged hole.
No matter how far from fulfilment they fell,
They picked themselves up in the vale where we dwell.

I wrap my old age in the warmth of each voice,
The shadows have fled and my heart can rejoice.
That the tape of their lives will forever unwind
On the spool of my thoughts, in the vaults of my mind,
For I was their friend and I shared troubled hours,
That time cannot bury 'neath crosses and flowers;
And waves of affection that nothing can quell,
Wash over me still in the vale where we dwell.

The green grass has grown o'er the black scars of man,
The slagheap has gone that engulfed Aberfan.
From Treharris to Dowlais, dead steelworks and mines
Stand guard with the past down wrecked railway lines.
Through sorrow and laughter the vision unfolds,
We live with the dream that the memory holds.
Undying the flame that transfigures the shell
Of Merthyr my town, in the vale where we dwell.

~ ~ ~ ~ ~ ~ ~

SOMEONE WHO IS ME

I never thought I'd welcome utter darkness as a friend,
And yet since I've been blind I've come to see,
That the world of my remembrance is a world that has no end,
Except the end of someone, who was me.

It matters less than nothing now, that rainbows have been drowned
In pools of emptiness that were my eyes,
For I can chase the colours that in my soul abound,
A spectrum that's reborn as vision dies.

In the glory of my childhood, when earth and flesh were one,
I scanned the new dimensions of my mind.
Where cells that stored great wonders, like the rising of the sun,
Created new beginnings I designed.

I knew my sight was fading, so I drained life's golden streams
And mixed them with the earth's primeval mud.
Then splashed it on a canvas in the garden of my dreams,
And signed it in the colour of my blood.

When stygian dark engulfed me and my world was one of touch,
The colours fell upon me just like rain;
While shades of countless flowers through my open pores would rush,
To telegraph their glory to my brain.

I cannot see my parents now, yet somehow just the same,
In some strange way they're closer than before.
They warm their voices on my love and as they speak my name
I see them both through childhood's open door.

I haven't shut myself away, the grass still knows my tread,
Although I seldom care to visit grief;
And never enter graveyards in the kingdom of the dead,
But live within the promise that is life.

Because there's still so much to do, and with time rushing by,
I try to push the dawn and dark apart;
And never let a moment pass or living hour die,
Until it's stamped its record on my heart.

My greatest joy is music poured from some celestial bowl,
For then I know why God created man,
And grafted inspiration onto his immortal soul,
As part of some harmonious global plan.

I never thought to take the dark as some men take a wife,
But in so many ways I've come to see,
That the road through my remembrance is a journey into life
And not the end of someone who is me.

~ ~ ~ ~ ~ ~ ~

DEWI DAVIS

Dewi Davis, (Dinas Powis),
Daffy picked the dilly fields.
Barmy bundled, flowered harvest,
That the mist moist, top soil yields.
Gold on green stalk, like his flowers,
Dewi Davis, Dinas Powis.

Like a clock his every movement,
Every second has to count.
Each day comes with some improvement,
As the seasons change about.
Like his gold watch, never slow is,
Dewi Davis, Dinas Powis.

Early rising, rainy morning,
Greasy slippers, slippery grass.
Sliding slowly through the dawning,
Where the moss on meadows mass.
Graceful gliding, where the plough is,
Dewi Davis, Dinas Powis.

Rich in bright gold, formed in petals,
Veiled in vase, or button-holed.
Nearer God than precious metals,
Radiantly their hearts unfold.
As he sees them happy now is,
Dewi Davis, Dinas Powis.

Dewi Davis, (Dinas Powis),
Daffy digs, the dilly soil.
Bulb implanting, all he knows is,
Spring is spun from winter toil.
May the poor folk in their houses,
May the rich men and their spouses,
May the whole world know his prowess,
Gold like daffodils he grows is,
Dewi Davis, Dinas Powis.

One day soon old age will trap him,
Where the yellow daffies sway.
Touch his stem and tender snap him,
For some long St. David's Day.
Then we'll see what time will show is,
Where he rests a golden glow is,
Where life's waters kiss the shore is,
Pride of Wales where death's wind blows is,
Dewi Davis, Dinas Powis.

~ ~ ~ ~ ~ ~ ~

AND NOT ON HILLS OF JOY

We've watched a nation's anguish, at the war in Vietnam.
We've seen their high hopes vanish, and we never gave a damn.
America, the brave and free, has been the whipping boy,
But they fought deep in misery, and not on hills of joy.

Their leaders were mistaken, and their people paid in blood,
And children died forgotten in that ceaseless gory flood.
Yet nations have a conscience, and this people deeply grieved,
While critics spouting nonsense poured their scorn and disbelieved.

From Pacific to Atlantic, as the shattered men returned,
The myth that war's romantic, was a lesson soon unlearned.
In Arlington the bugles blew, o'er coffins draped in flags,
While arms wholesalers' profits drew, as peasants walked in rags.

This wasn't just a simple war, with battle lines clear drawn,
You fought the troops your tired eyes saw, and wished yourself unborn,
As all around you, Viet Cong, their treacherous ambush planned,
To spring unseen, so lithe and strong, like countless grains of sand.

They say the big battalions come victorious out of war,
But weaklings fight like stallions, if the cause they're fighting for
Invokes within the human frame, a light in the gathering dark,
That springs to an immortal flame, from life's eternal spark.

If all the blood this war has spilled, ran red toward the sea,
And all the men the guns have killed, through this war's history,
Were placed before our consciences, like canvas in a frame,
No artist born could colour it, or give the daub a name.

For this horror can't be painted, no brush can sketch in death,
And the ones who watch are tainted by the artist's very breath.
The human landscape, sombrely, sweeps endless like the waves,
While painted men, like you and me, march onward to their graves.

O Christ, our great Redeemer, look down with love on us,
On soldier boy and dreamer, who in thy mercy trust.
Smooth with thine hand this tortured earth, and wipe all war away,
That we might know the peaceful birth, of God's awakening day.

And to great, proud, America, give that which is thine own,
A depth of soul, a guiding star, that leads to thee alone.
And give us understanding, in a world that's filled with pain,
That we might undemanding walk, thy true straight path again.

~ ~ ~ ~ ~ ~ ~

THE CORNERSTONE OF HEAVEN

High on a hilltop lies a man the world should mourn,
He wasn't president or king, except within his home.
But through the years of pain that made his life,
He lived for his dear children, home, and wife.

His mission was, to all intents, a simple one,
Yet 'tis by simple, striving, men that noble deeds are done.
And when his story's writ in golden script above,
It will be seen that every line, contains the word of love.
He sang us lullabies and though he had no voice,
The feeling would have made a nightingale rejoice.
I hear you still my father, singing down the years,
As though your love still tries to brush away the tears.

He worked down filthy shafts, that we might burn the coal,
Depleting stores of health in some forsaken hole.
Scorched by wind and sun and soaked by winter's rain,
The years dug furrows through his flesh to sow the seeds of pain.

His strength was like a hill, yet even hills erode,
And no man born should bear the brunt of such a load.
Though suffering was his lot, we never saw him cry,
He did it all for us, and never questioned why.

Within my callow heart, when all my world was dreams,
He loosed a flood of thought in one continuous stream.
Remembering inside him the magic haunts of youth,
And trying in his wisdom to help me find the truth.

I never heard him swear, of drink the brewers curse,
His lungs were shot to hell, though smoking made them worse.
The pleasures that he took, were always given free
And comradeship he shared, still makes a friend of me.

He lived his life through empty nights and haunted workless days,
When men despaired and went their own despairing ways.
Yet still he smiled within his broken valley tomb,
Lighting up the hearts of those encompassed in the gloom.

High on a hilltop lies a man the world has lost,
Facing down the valley where his wandering footsteps crossed.
And deep inside the hearts of those who loved him best
The hill is ever sacred where this man is laid to rest.

You are not forgotten my dear father, nor have your smiles faded away, While I live, while I breathe I will remember you. And when my heart is lonely, I will reach out and embrace all the golden memories we shared, and I will find again the cornerstone of Heaven!

MY VALLEY RIVER

Flow through time, my valley river,
Wind from birth through life to death.
Leap and pulse to course forever
Through my blood, my bone, my breath.
Come past daffodils on meadows,
Come black cloaked through hills of coal,
Come through light and valley shadows,
To that sea within my soul.

As my skin your freshness touches,
I am cleansed of life's foul grime,
Borne refreshed past singing rushes
Through the vale that runs through time.
As your rippling pools surround me,
As this lovely land unfolds,
Mountain ramparts mass around me,
To their strength my spirit holds.

Burst from springs through rocky fissures,
Fall from hill down craggy slope,
Meet and mate in bed of rivers,
Whence is born the stream of hope.
Torrent rush through channels narrow
Join with brooks thy bosom feeds,
Through my bones be thou the marrow
From my flesh be thou the seeds.

As my dreaming thoughts awaken,
As the call of home I feel,
In my mem'ry I am taken,
Child again that thou can'st heal,
Could I by your sweet banks tarry,
Feel communion with your source,
Wales and heart would mate and marry,
Where your tumbling waters course.

Dress the earth with green, my river,
Pleasure those who love thee most.
To parched throats be thou the giver,
To thy teeming life, be host.
Come past fields of sighing grasses,
Come grim faced through beds of coal,
Go where joy in living passes
To that sea within my soul.

~ ~ ~ ~ ~ ~ ~

DOUBLE JOINTED LEGS

In a level through a mountain just this side of Aberdare
You will find fantastic creatures that Dai Lloyd's collected there
There are scientists from Mercury and clever frogs from Mars,
And strange misshapen spiders from the nearest of the stars.

They are gathered down this level just to find the reason why
The Welsh steam coal they're mining there is causing folk to die,
Not only here where it is burned, but on the planets too,
As holes in space around our world let deadly gasses through.

On Venus folk are turning square from their triangular shape,
And as their doors have just three sides, from homes they can't escape
While up on Mars canals are full of suicides and such,
For since the gasses clogged their pores they've lost their sense of touch.

On Jupiter the crops have failed, on Mercury the bees
Have grown as big as elephants, and pollinate the trees,
Not with the seeds of living fruit, but with some fungoid plant
That decimates the bark and leaves and makes the tree trunks slant.

On Saturn, rings of shining ice, are riddled now with flaws,
While Pluto's doglike ruling race are frothing round their jaws.
The asteroids are breaking up, the moon is turning green,
And on the stars, its got so dark, they can't see where they've been.

So Dai and all his motley crew work hard to make it pass
That Welsh steam coal will burn without its deadly poison gas.
While scientists from Mercury and Martian frogs with brains,
Crush anthracite to powdered dust and analyse the grains.

These bug-eyed monsters from the stars now lodge in Aberdare,
With Liza Jenkins, Bronwen Pugh and Vanoo (Gelligaer)
They're far from home and starved of love, and so you may expect,
That there will be strange children born if they go on unchecked.

Already, one has wed Meg. Price, and her the whole town shuns,
For as he is Venusian they'll have triangular sons.
But even worse, the Martian frog who's courting Mary Beggs,
Has got two heads, revolving eyes, and double jointed legs.

They've formed a bug-eyed Rugby team, these things from outer space,
But as they've got advantages denied the human race,
Like multi legs with twelve toed feet we know the reason why
They always win the ball from scrums and score so many tries.

Perhaps their offspring born down here will one day play for Wales,
Though some will look like worker ants and some like garden snails.
We're not that fussy how they look, it's how they play that counts,
And no-one here will criticise, if they can England trounce.

But now I hear they've formed a choir and they're Eisteddfod bound,
And if you've ever heard them sing you know how bad they sound.
For most have voices pitched so deep the earth is made to shake
From Barry Island in the south right up to Bala lake.

There's havoc caused in social clubs each time a drink they call,
For most of them have triple mouths and stand quite ten feet tall.
And by the time one mouth is reached (I'll swear that this is true),
There's extra hands, a pint in each, raised to the other two.

But no-one picks a fight with them, not since John Williams died,
They'll not forgive an insult made, they're very strong on pride
For some mad creature from the stars whom John had joked about,
Plunged tentacles right down his throat and pulled him inside out.

It's no good going to the law, to question or complain,
For all who work on Dai Lloyd's team have been absolved from blame.
By governments down here on earth, who need their expert aid
To purify the noxious fumes of which they're so afraid.

And so the level through the hill, this side of Aberdare,
Is full of monsters, most bug-eyed, who crush the steam coal there.
Not with machines but with their jaws, or maybe with their feet,
For when you weigh two metric tons, that's quite a lot of meat.

On Venus they're still turning square, on Mars canals are packed,
While Pluto's dog-like ruling race are hydrophobia wracked,
The Martian frogs are turning pink, Mercurian spiders puce,
While creatures from the nearer stars are running out of juice.

It looks as if Dai's mining team will have to work apace,
To solve the problems posed by gas, polluting outer space.
Or one by one good folk will die, and girls like Mary Beggs,
Will marry four eyed Martian frogs, with double jointed legs.

~ ~ ~ ~ ~ ~ ~

REFLECTS AN IMAGE

Not lightly, but with heavy heart, I write these bitter lines
Yet I sincerely wish there was no cause.
For I who murdered bright ideals, know no aspirant climbs
To any shining peak unmarred by flaws.
I would that it were otherwise, the mirror to my soul,
Reflects an image no true eye should see,
And nothing that I've ever done, or all the power I hold,
Will ever change the image that is me.

It seems like only yesterday when first I trod the road
That led not to the stars but to the dark.
More able men I trampled on, for I could not afford
To go through life and never make my mark.

No loving kindness have I shown, no friendships have I made,
Relationships were luxuries I barred,
And children's voices begging for attention as they played,
Were blunted by my total disregard.

I changed the course of many lives, trailed ruin in my wake,
And shook no hand that could not smooth my way.
Used people I cared nothing for (except to watch them break)
Then left their crippled feelings where they lay.
The heights were scaled, but at a price that left no room for love,
The levers that could move the world were mine.
And carelessly I handled them with such a brutish touch,
The walls of hope and trust were undermined.

Not lightly, but with utter truth, I state what is my case,
Not in defence, but simply to explain,
That I who murdered tenderness must at my judgement face
A sentence that is fashioned out of pain.
I wish that it were otherwise, the mirror to my mind
Reflects ambition no true eye should see,
And nothing that I now could do, or reason I could find
Will ever change the image that is me.

~ ~ ~ ~ ~ ~ ~

PORTHCAWL

There on the sands, miles of naked flesh showing,
Pink as spun candyfloss, red as mint rock.
Children with spade and pail, sandcastles growing
Wives in bikinis and husbands in shock.

Young couples sparking with canvas chairs swaying,
Lost in youths dream and the stripes on their seat.
Forgetting the world or the sky in its greying,
For this is their moment and time is so fleet.

Grandads on yesterday's memories browsing
Rheumy old eyes on the proud jutting breasts.
Sliding down curves but their thoughts not arousing
Fire to the blood at mad passions unguessed.

Middle-aged couples with unmarried daughters
Old enough now to leave parents on sands
And flirt with their eyes as they come to close quarters
With pimply young men bearing juice in their glands.

Boarding House keepers on their best behaviour,
Welsh accents masked by veneers varnished on.
Booking you in as if doing a favour,
And counting their profits before you are gone.

Shopkeepers selling their seaside mementos,
Tawdry bright gifts brushed with silver and gilt.
Greengrocer stalls with their salad tomatoes,
And bunches of flowers that tiredly wilt.

Neighbours and friends from your town or your village,
Glad to shout greetings from high promenade.
Sharing a love that the world can't diminish,
Waves of emotion on streams of regard.

Coney Beach swallowing pleasure bent children,
Digesting them all in its iron insides.
Then spewing them into a neon lit cauldron,
On vinegar rivers and fish and chip tides.

Wild windy corner of Sunday School outings,
Long may you buffet the great and the small.
Whip off their hats and then carry their shoutings
To echo forever in timeless Porthcawl.

~ ~ ~ ~ ~ ~ ~

THE SWEET POOL OF YOUTH

The child looked at me, from her sweet pool of youth,
To see on the map of my face,
The journey through age to the country of truth,
Redemption, oblivion, disgrace.
The fields in her eyes were a daffodil gold,
The smoothness of charm was her skin.
The curve of her lips was vermillion and bold,
Sweet frame for the laughter within.

She reached up and touched all the worry and care,
The furrows and hills of my brow.
Brushed fingertips soft through the snow of my hair,
God knows, how it comes to me now!
She'd ask my forgiveness for some foolish act,
O grandchild to ask this of me!
May the tears of my soul, from the springs of my heart,
Pour out as a blessing on thee.

The sweet pool of youth has dried in her eyes,
Along with the daffodil gold.
She'll never yet age, or ever grow wise,
The lips and the young flesh are cold.
And the map of my face shows the treasure has gone,
While the cross at its heart is a grave.
Through the snow of my hair as her touch lingers on,
I'll remember the sweet love she gave.

Sometime, as I walk through the valley of pain,
The hills of her joy mass around;
Then just for a moment I see her again,
Where the paths to her fragrance abound.
Unseeing I stare at the world that is mine,
While the bitterness all flows away.
I have knelt, I have sipped, at the pool that is wine,
I have lived to the end of the day.

To the end of the day, I have lived, my friends,
The darkness is not far away.
I know she is waiting where my journey ends,
And I know the dear words she'll say.

The seeds that we sow are full long in the ground,
But the flower is waiting to rise,
And when it is plucked then the way will be found
To the daffodil fields in her eyes.

- By the sweet pool of youth, where that child looked at me,
From the daffodil fields in her eyes.

~ ~ ~ ~ ~ ~ ~

WITH WRITHING WREATHS

The soil was soiled by muddy mud,
The fields were fouled by bloody blood.
The burning barbs of wounding wire,
Were dressed with death by field gun fire.

The shattered shafts of treasured trees,
Stood guard like gods with knotty knees
While whistling wind from shooting shell,
Blew many men and boys to hell.

Death's ghoulish ghost grinned grisly glad,
On godly good and beastly bad.
To foully fold in dark dislike,
The bristling brave and meek alike.

The salty searing tears of truth,
From sullied souls poured yet on youth.
To weep the waste of manly mind,
And cleanse the conscience of mankind.

The hate that hides in burning breast,
Brings haunted hours and grief unguessed.
Brings heroes home with splintered bones,
And leaves the dead rot under stones.

The cuckoo clock that leaped eleven,
Brought silence down like balm from Heaven.
Too ling'ring late to salve and save,
The shattered soldier in his grave.

At Cenotaphs, the leaders lunge,
With writhing wreaths, as if to sponge
The muddy mud and bloody blood,
From battle field and poppy bud.

In sombre suits from Savile Row,
They soulless sing and maudlin grow.
The proudly promise rule of law,
Prosperity and end to war.

O Loving Lord, shut lying lips,
And dry with dust the drool that drips,
Raise ladders long for saintly soul,
That they might flee this Devil's hole.

Give perfect peace to world that waits,
And freedom for stormtrooper states.
Cleanse wounding wire of festered flesh,
Wipe filth from fields and farrow fresh.

Thus shattered stumps of trunkless trees,
Will saplings send to brace the breeze,
And shrapnel shorn from shooting shell,
Will rootless rust where honour fell.

And muddy mud and bloody blood,
Will soil no soil or poppy bud.

~ ~ ~ ~ ~ ~ ~ ~

SUNDAY SCHOOL OUTING 1932

"Its Barry as usual this year, I suppose",
Said Jonas the Hill, with a tug at his nose.
"The G.W.R give a good party rate,
If we get them off early and don't leave too late".
But Thomas (Stone Chippings) who kept all our cash,
Went red in the face and came out in a rash.
"Cheap rate or not, with our Sunday School funds,
We can hardly afford some of John Morgan's buns.

It's Pontsarn or nothing, and nothing's more like,
Unless the men walk and the boys go by bike.
The women and babies can travel by train,
And Donkins (The Gout) by wheelchair again.
At Chapel next Sunday we want volunteers,
If no-one comes forward then any old dears,
To pack picnic lunches and make some small beer,
And I might as well tell you now that you're all here,
That we don't want a repeat of the of the social in May
When Dai (Organ Chest) sang his rude songs all day,
And collapsed on the pulpit as drunk as a lord,
To be found two days later by my Auntie Maud,
Who was putting some beeswax where beeswax should go,
Tripped over Dai's body full length on the floor,
And though he went Temperance by signing the pledge
There's still empty bottles behind his front hedge.
So remember it's small beer and not parsnip wine
The minister's wife has eyesight so fine,
She can tell at a mile who stands and who falls,
And whose aim is straight at the coconut stalls.
Remember last year when Danny Full Pelt,
Left his trousers undone and fell over his belt,
And tripped with his head falling into her lap,
And he didn't wear pants or a vest or a cap.
I can still hear her screams as she saw his bare back,
A lovely white rump but all the rest black
Fresh from his shift down the pit Danny was
And he was the stone that had gathered no moss.

I'll never quite know what his own doctor wrote
But Danny Full Pelt never came up in court;
And I'll tell you again while my memory's fresh,
That the sermon for weeks was the sins of the flesh,
Young Mary Pugh's conscience was troubled so bad
That she spilled all the beans about Tom to her dad,
And was married in August with corset so tight,
She had to stop breathing to marry in white.
Still a fine set of twins she had for all that,

November it was and she was rather fat,
And Danny Full Pelt and the minister's wife
Were both at the Christening, larger than life.
And the moral to that while we're all gathered here,
Is leave parsnip wine and stick to small beer.

There's no harm in pickles, red cabbage, or beet,
We'll take liver sausage, we can't afford meat.
Brown bread and white and best margarine,
Ten per cent butter, we can't be too mean.
Bread pudding and rock cakes but not Liza Jane's.
God couldn't find her when handing out brains.
You'd think that she'd know with self raising flour,
You don't put in yeast every hour on the hour.
It took two strong men working hard half the night,
To open the oven, the door was so tight,
And when they'd broke through, the strange thing inside,
Sank into their souls, and both of them cried.
Good men they've both been from that day to this,
They never give Sunday night chapel a miss.
When you've witnessed the worst the Devil can do
You know there's a heaven when life's journey is through.
So Morgan's good wife can supply all our cakes
She uses fresh eggs and best lard when she bakes.
I'm sure she teaches those hens in her yard,
The best eggs to lay to blend with the lard.
Brown sugar for toffee, but not Demerara,
We've tried that before and it melts in hot weather.
We don't want Twm Dido's two boys stuck to walls,
We daren't show our faces again in Porthcawl.
The minister's wife is past calculating
What the Chapel's still paying for redecorating,
Twelve inches of skin those two flamers lost,
And twelve rolls of paper we've paid to our cost.
Perhaps we should stick to boiled sweets and fruit,
Remind me to wear just my second best suit.
No good taking chances with children like ours,
Thank God! there's no gardens with rose trees and flowers.

Just a field, and a hut if it comes on to rain
(We'll have to ask Idwal to clean out the drain)
The last time we used it, it smelled of old socks
And I got sharp looks till we found that dead fox.
We'll send Mrs Parry the Wednesday before
To put some Jeyes fluid all over the floor.
A lovely strong smell that do give when it's ripe
It's almost like smoking rubbed flake in my pipe.
I know that my wife when she's had a good dose,
Goes right off her snuff and blocks up her nose".

Lew Pritchard the Chemist, check suited and gruff,
Was full to the gills and had heard quite enough.
He rapped on the table and climbed to his feet,
And said; "Oh to hell with the Sunday School treat.
The Pendarren End has been open an hour
And all you can talk of is self raising flour.
I move we adjourn or take up a vote,
I've got all of twenty dry frogs in my throat.
I know that we all think much better on beer
And anything's better than just sitting here.
It's Band of Hope soon and Sisterhood after,
And Thomas (Stone Chippings) gets dafter and dafter".

The meeting broke up as they both came to blows,
With Pritchard the Chemist quite light on his toes.
They circled the table and trod on my feet
And Thomas (Stone Chippings) was boxing a treat,
When who should walk in but the minister's wife,
I'll remember that scene for the rest of my life.
Just one look she gave and we all turned to stone
Oh why do we harvest the crop we have sown.
Sufficient to say that from that day to this
We give all the Sunday School outings a miss.

~ ~ ~ ~ ~ ~ ~

THE BEGINNING

GENESIS   Chapter One

This was the great beginning, the start of all we know,
When heaven and earth were joined as one, because God willed it so.
The void was dark and formless, wrapped in a shroud of death
As God the Holy Spirit came with His life-giving breath.

"Let there be light" the Maker said, and lo! the light shone forth,
Divided from the black of space by Heaven's almighty force.
And God He named the darkness night, and light He called the day,
As on Creation's troubled breast, the shade and radiance lay.

Between the waters that He formed, God made a great divide,
To separate the air from sea, and this He called the sky.
The borders of the day He moved as sky its waters shed,
And thus the second morning passed, and there the evening fled.

God moved the waters of the sea beyond the golden strand,
And all the earth exposed by this He gave the name of land.
He looked to where the great waves rolled and where the mountains stood,
To see the Eden that He made, and knew that it was good.

The God enriched emerging land, producing trees and vines,
Vegetation, plants and seeds of many different kinds.
And as God marvelled at His world and saw that it would last,
The third day came just a He planned and so the hours passed.

The great expanse of empty sky was studded now with lights,
A ball of fire to warm the days, the moon and stars for nights.
They marked the seasons as they sped, they measured all the days,
So shone the sky on this fourth night, and God was filled with praise.

He made the creatures in the sea, and birds that soared on high,
And two He made of all of them in water and in sky.
He gave a blessing to them all, their numbers to increase,
And there was morning, and evening too, it was the fifth of these.

And God said "Let the land bring forth, creatures that crawl and run,
Tame and wild to roam the earth, and different every one."
He formed them all to fit His plan, no others would He make,
For life was His alone to give and His alone to take.

He spun the globe that was the Earth, and knew that it was fair,
Saw plants and trees that bore much fruit, saw land and sea and air.
Observed the oceans' teeming life, the graceful birds that flew,
With all the livestock of the world, and all the seeds that grew.

And God He said "Let's now make Man an image unto me,
In my own special likeness cast, that he might master be
Of every fish and every bird, and all the beasts that crawl,
For him I make to crown my works, and he will rule them all."

So make and female did He form, and perfect were they made,
The mirror image of their God and in His flesh arrayed.
He laid a blessing on them both and bade them multiply,
To fill the earth with all their heirs that man might never die.

"Rule over fish and fowl and beast" the great Creator said,
"You are the chosen of this world and I will keep you fed.
I'll give you every seed and plant and every fruitful tree,
For everything that lives is yours, and you belong to me."

God saw the wonder that He wrought, for perfect was His touch,
The plan fulfilled just as He willed and so He loved it much.
And as the sun moved through the hours to in the darkness fade,
The sixth creative day was done and earth a garden made.

Thus did Creation come to pass, and as the seventh dawn came,
God made of it a day of rest and Sabbath was its name.
He clothed its light in holiness, He filled its dark with prayer,
Where Man could walk and talk with God and of His mercy share.

THE OLD GREAT WESTERN LINE

Flashing past my carriage windows,
On the old Great Western Line,
Engine steam the rushing wind blows
Half obscures this land of mine.
We have come from Cardiff Central,
On our journey up the Taff,
And we'er bound for Merthyr Tydfil
On a rising, curving, graph.

We will call at Cardiff Queen Street,
Llandaff, Radyr and Taffs Well.
Then at both Treforest stations
Looking like the gates of hell.
The sluggish river putrefies,
With foul industrial waste,
As our locomotive bustles by
With quite indecorous haste.

We will change our train at Ponty,
This one goes to Aberdare,
But they're bound to have one handy,
By the time that we reach there.
We will look down where the road drops,
To the town below the bridge,
We will cast our eyes past roof tops,
To that Needle on the ridge.

Our next stop is Abercynon,
Prompting Mam to say again,
As she sees the station coming
Through the misty valley rain,
"I was born just past that lamp-post,
In the cottage that you see",
And you'd think to hear our Mam boast,
That a mansion it must be.

We will climb the wooded gradient,
To our stop at Quakers Yard,
And then onward to Mount Pleasant
Past the hillsides torn and scarred.

The Merthyr Vale (for Aberfan)
Where pit wheel starkly spins,
And slag heaps poise to wait for man
To lose what coal dust wins.

We have come from Cardiff Central
On our journey up the Taff.
And we're bound for Merthyr Tydfil,
Through the Halt at Pentrebach.
Flashing past my carriage windows
From that childhood world of mine,
Come the images that time blows
Down the old Great Western Line.

~ ~ ~ ~ ~ ~ ~

SAY NOT THIS WILL HAPPEN

Say not this is England as we in future years
Gaze on grassless meadows with eyes that fill with tears.
Speak not then of songbirds in hedgerows decked for Spring,
For that which lives in memory has no sweet song to sing.

Climb not barren mountains, where once the green fern curled
And barbed leaf yellow gorse adorned the rooftop of our world.
Avoid once gentle hollows that sheltered from the storms
The timid sheep the years have changed to strange mutated forms.

Fish not poisoned waters, for somewhere in those deeps
The last survivor, scaleless now, just lies but never sleeps.
Perhaps its mind still active, dreams its timeless dream
Wherein the murky waters part with ghosts of trout and bream.

Walk not into forests, for leaf and branch are dead
And tall trees ossified to stone, stand guard like troops of lead.
Where slime primeval oozes forth where once green mosses clung,
And native squirrels leap no more where nuts and berries hung.

Gather in no harvest, of others or your own,
The radio-active bitter earth has poisoned all that's sown.
The years that saw atomic waste processed in dreaming shires,
Are lit by blue unearthly light from vast consuming fires.

Turn your gaze not heavenward, the once eternal stars
Are cloaked by leaden petrol fumes from fifty billion cars.
No doubt the silver shining moon around our globe still spins
But hidden now from watching eyes by cloud that never thins.

Speak not now of Bethlehem, the babe will not be born
For how can God give Christ to them who curtained off the dawn.
Jerusalem, Jerusalem I hear the faithful cry
As He who gave us hope to live now gives us time to die.

Say not this is England, as we roll back through time,
To light our fires in wattle huts on stilts above the slime.
Speak not now of songbirds or to your memory cling
The rough, foul beasts that roam the earth have no sweet song to sing!

~ ~ ~ ~ ~ ~ ~

THE UPLAND SLOPES

Each new morn I'd wake and say,
This is the great, the glorious day.
This is the day to stride out strong,
To the distant hills where I belong.
I'd look to the window, framed by blue,
Where the Brecknock Beacons beckoned through,
And feel inside a million thrills,
Pulsed to life by the upland hills;
Where mournful winds and mountain sheep,
Keen the slopes where the old gods sleep.
Where Romans marched and wild Celt fought,
Where Normans found what Saxons sought.
Where farmers's sons with cheeks like wine,
Plodded south to mill and mine,
Where country lungs choked hard on dust,
And ploughshares oxidised to rust.
Where fathers grieved on hillside farms,
And old, young, girls mourned empty arms.
Where blackthorn hedge and limestone wall,
Marched in step with fir trees tall;

And wild flower rainbows in the grass,
Colour the lives of those who pass.
Oh! to return to the long lost hopes,
Of life and love on the upland slopes.
But here I lie on this crisp, cold morn,
The years in ruin, the body worn.
Tell tale scars of blue on my face,
Palms black grimed with the earths disgrace.
The wine long drained from my country cheeks,
Hoist with the petard the wanderer seeks.
My broken dreams in Time's lost sleep,
Engulfed by nightmares memory keeps,
Of morning shifts with sun and skies,
Kept by the coal from my longing eyes;
Of the dread in my heart as the pit-cage sank,
To the grisly depths so cold and dank,
Where I'd sell my soul for a bird's sweet song,
High on the hills where my heart beat strong.
Where the muffled rain on the yellow gorse
And the unshod hooves of the mountain horse,
Thrum to the music of waterfalls,
And the whistling sounds of the shepherd calls,
With the answering bark of the faithful dog
Guiding the sheep through the valley fog,
Home to the farmhouse, weathered and strong,
Where the heart ad the soul and mind belong.
Oh! to return to the upland slopes
And to live again the long lost hopes.

Yes, this is the day to stride out strong,
But my legs are stiff and the road is long.
I'll bury my pit clothes deep in the dust,
And wear again what a hill man must.
I'll say goodbye to my collier friends,
And take the road where the river bends;
Up past the graveyard high on the hill,
Where my Sarah lies and always will.
Where my tears have flowed full many a day,
Mourning the love that has passed away.
Past the tiny mound where our daughter Jean

Hides away from what might have been,
When the world was young and she was all,
And my Sarah nursed her in her shawl.
But what God gives, He takes away,
And Sarah's heart was broke that day;
And I look to the Beacons beckoning through
My bedroom window framed by blue,
And the million thrills are thrills no more,
As I lie on this bed as I've lain before,
To feel again as the twilight falls,
The closing in of these mean bare walls,
And know again the death of hopes
Of life and love on the upland slopes.

~ ~ ~ ~ ~ ~ ~

THIS WORLD'S PAIN

Where my immortal spirit soars
There are no prison walls or doors
But only unconfining space
Where mind and soul can grow in grace.

Through this world's eyes my flight is vain,
They see me lie on couch of pain,
Not knowing that which sets me free
Is more than mortal eye can see.

For I inherit from the Word,
The sweetest music man has heard,
As golden trumpets bravely blow
From God to me in ceaseless flow.

As fevered flesh must restless toss,
I look past pain and see the cross,
To know that perfect man once died,
That I might in God's heaven abide.

No earthly bonds can hold me fast,
I go into His arms at last;
And all that I have suffered here,
Is naught as paradise draws near.

And this I know through my belief,
That this world's pain and this life's grief,
Will pass away at Heaven's doors,
Where my immortal spirit soars.

~ ~ ~ ~ ~ ~ ~

YOU LOOK LIKE THE CHAP

ly goodness" said Dai, "It's boiling down here"
As doomed he came to the portals of hell.
"It's just the place for a tankard of beer
And maybe a chaser of scotch as well.
If this is the place where colliers retire
Who cuts all the coal for this roaring fire?"

"Hello" said the Devil, as Dai walked in,
"You look like the chap that we're invoice for,
Gravelly lungs and blue scarred skin
Muscular back and a granite jaw.
There's a six foot seam of the best Welsh coal
Waiting for you down that bottomless hole".

"My word" said our Dai, hurt to the quick
"I'm all worked out and my body's worn.
For forty-five years I've swung my pick
Until I ache in my every bone.
There's been a mistake, I should have been blessed
And sent to Heaven for a bit of rest".

"There's no mistake", said the Devil with glee,
"I asked for Dai and Dai is your name.
You fit my requirements down to a tee
And you've only your sinful life to blame.
With half of your valley sinning so well
Be glad that it's you that I've chosen for hell".

"Dammo!", said Dai, as his words sank in,
"You asked for a Dai and a Dai you've got,
But up in our valley besides the sin
There's far more blokes called Dai than not.
You've got the wrong Dai and the Dai you want,
Is the Dai Small Coal who lives up the Bont".

"That may be so", the old Devil wheezed,
"But he's still alive, which you Dai are not,
And all in all I'm really quite pleased
With the kind of Dai that I think I've got.
So rather than waiting for Dai Small Coal
You're cutting the seam in that bottomless hole".

So down in the cage our Dai was sent
Cursing away as old colliers will,
Protesting his innocence as he went
And for all I know he's down there still.
So the moral's plain - if you're Dai as well
Change your name quick or you'll go to hell!

~ ~ ~ ~ ~ ~ ~

ON GOLD HILL FARM

We picked the hops on Gold Hill Farm,
Not far from lovely Ledbury.
We lived in stalls above a barn
And shopped in quaint old Bosbury.
The farmyard smells were frankincense,
The green slimed ponds were silver lakes,
The climb to fragrant residence,
Were steps a childhood dreamer takes.

The cooking shed, with iron fire,
Lay past cowpattied, mucky, yard,
Where I was piggy-backed through mire,
On my dad's back, so strong and hard.

He lit the fire with red tipped match,
And used his cap to fan the flame,
While sweat dropped from his curly thatch,
To boil and hiss on red hot frame.

The kettle boiled on blackened hook,
And as my father made the tea,
I watched his old contented look,
As he stood towering over me.
Italian plum tomatoes tipped,
With loving care from garish can,
While strips of smoky bacon crisped,
In sizzling fat, in frying pan.

Around us in their various stalls,
The other families broke their fast,
And even in baronial halls,
They could not equal this repast.
Our table tops were tea chest lids,
We sat on logs that held our beds,
Farm mesmerised, enchanted, kids,
With magic brewing, in our heads.

And O! that lovely, hopyard smell,
The bitter tang, with sulphur nipped.
The wondrous scent that cast a spell,
That through my life, has held, and gripped.
The bine spaced lanes were golden gates,
That led to child-hood paradise,
A special place where memory waits,
To flash remembrance, to the eyes.

Throughout the day, the tradesmen called,
And we small children, gladly went,
Where brash fish-monger stood, and bawled,
And reeked of his decaying scent,
Or spent a penny where the van
Of ice-creamed joy awaited us,
Or bought some toffee from the man,
Who served us from converted bus.

With penny bloaters, fried in lard,
We ate our chunks of bread and marge.
The fish was cheap, the crusts were hard,
The price was small, the portions, large.
With hopstained hands we cleaned our plates,
Until the last small crumb had gone,
Then sat around on empty crates,
To munch Welsh-cakes or toasted scone.

Such days come back alive with joy,
To fill my soul with sweet desire,
That I might be again a boy,
To join that circle round the fire;
To watch my lovely father, while
He laughed his way through ancient joke,
Or see my mam's contented smile,
Through kettle's steam, or green wood smoke.

They come with love from happier days,
These sweet tipped arrows from the past;
To pierce our hearts in tender ways,
Where joy and sorrow, merge at last.
The living know, there is no death,
The family circle, nowhere yields,
And we avow with every breath,
The love we shared, in hopyard fields.

In hopyard fields, green hopyard fields,
Where memory her power wields,
To recreate the joy that yields,
The harvest, love, in hopyard fields.

THE GLORY THAT SHONE

Memory powers the time machine
That takes back the heart where childhood has been.
Where love was a candle and joy was its flame,
And magic was ours as each Christmas day came.

The singing of carols in yesterday's streets,
The iceblock of time that my memory defeats.
The faith born of glory in old Bethlehem
From seed that was sown by the maker of men.

I still hear us singing those carols of old,
Our young voices blending in silver and gold.
Sometimes in darkness and sometimes in light,
But always together as we scaled the heights.

We sang out of gladness in perfect accord,
Of that wondrous baby, our Saviour and Lord.
And prayed that our listeners would drink of the stream
That we poured through their doors from the heart of our dream.

And as we returned we were never alone,
For One crowned by thorns walked with us to our home.
Wrapped in His glory and warmed by His love,
We soared on faith's wings to God's mansion above.

The Christ star will shine as it always has done,
For the birth of a Saviour, the gift of a Son.
Bringing bright angels with tidings sublime,
And wisemen with gifts from the reaches of time.

Thus memories sweet of Christmases past,
That flowed into dreams and vanished too fast.
Will all be remembered as we journey on
To Bethlehem town and the glory that shone.

So travel with me on my time machine,
Where grass on the field of remembrance is green.
Where innocence stirred in a soul undefiled,
And faith came alive in the heart of a child!

~ ~ ~ ~ ~ ~ ~

ONE IN A MILLION

A mother is someone whose children stay young, no matter how far
                                              they may stray,
Remembering she nursed them so long in her arms through many a
                                              dark troubled day.
Holding their tenderness close to her breast and feeling the miracle flood
That she was the giver of warmth to the flesh, the river of life to the blood.
Before they speak she knows what they'll say, the knowledge is older than time.
And so she responds to their every desire in ways that are almost sublime.
She takes them to school their very first day, she knows what this parting means,
As those who were babies in yesterday's pram, go off to a world that's unseen.
A mother is someone who can't be replaced, a mother is simply unique,
She was and she is and will be evermore for as long as we're able to speak.
There is no reward that we children can give, for all the greatness she is,
The waves of her caring break over life's rocks and fall on us all like a kiss.
She's songs from a hymn book, nurse upon call, doctor to most of our ills,
Tales told at bedtime, sheets that are cool, moonbeams on windows and sill.
Acres of washing bestraddling a line, soapsuds on work roughened hands,
Hours of toil to keep the home clean, a labour that living demands.
She's maker of welcomes, usher of dreams, planner of parties and fun,
Joy in an apron, smiles in the air, and words that are always goldspun.
She's one in a million, steadfast and true, processions of meals on a tray,
The end of a rainbow, showers of stars, light at the end of the day.
Self is a concept she doesn't embrace, it's others who always come first,
Ready to listen when troubles are told, believing the best not the worst.
Sometimes she worries but this she won't show, her face mustn't mirror her fears,
For she's the rock the house stands upon, that never will move thro' the years.
A mother is hope in a framework of trust, words that are never unkind,
The smoothing of ointment on grazes and scrapes, the soothing of
                                              doubt in the mind.
She's patience unending, laughter restored, tears just as precious as pearls,
The tug of a comb untangling hair, fingertips brushing through curls.
Poetry blending with self raising flour, pastry that melts on the tongue,
Tablecloth tapestries garnished with oils, sauces from paradise sprung.

A mother is silk in a cheap cotton dress, perfume in tablets of soap,
Charm beyond words in an old Sunday hat, blossom on garlands of hope.
The hiss of an iron on freshly damped clothes, gentleness trying to please.
Hands juggling dishes from table to sink, tiredness nobody sees.
Tendrils of hair escaping their bonds, sweat on a brow that's too warm,
Answers to questions in unending flow, peace in the eye of a storm.
Courage that's dragged from reserves in the soul, fortitude worlds without end,
A shoulder to cry on through life's deepest troughs, always the
                                                    first to befriend.
Someone who fears as anxiety mounts when children stay out far too late,
Sharing a prayer with a listening God who knows it is harder to wait.
A mother is hair changing slowly to white as the years multiply out of sight,
Aided by worry, sickness and age and loneliness felt in then night.
She longs to be wanted by those whom she loves, and sometimes when
                                                    she is alone.
She looks at chairs that are empty because her children have
                                                    homes of their own.
When bed-time approaches she fastens her doors, so she can feel safe in her bed,
But there are no locks to shut out the dreams that are memories
                                                    relived in her head.
It's now that she knows what the past was about, the day to day dramas of life,
The love of a husband, the trust of a child, the joy of a mother and wife.
She hasn't forgotten the struggles she had when facing the world with a smile,
But measures such times with happiness shared and finds it all was
                                                    worthwhile.
A mother is light in the gathering dark, a beacon that always will guide
Children and memories straight from the past to places prepared at her side.
Where all that is lovely can always be found, where all that is good can be felt,
A place in the heart that will always be warm, where the ice of our
                                                    worries can melt.
And as we sing praises for all that she is, we hope that the riches we share
Will fashion a garment of wonder and love that's fit for a mother to wear.

~ ~ ~ ~ ~ ~ ~

TWENTY YEAR, OR MORE

It's strange what tricks the memory
Plays on rememb'ring brain,
You'd think the past would settle now,
Not trouble me again.
But still I see, as if today,
Those firemen I knew,
Ride the same appliances,
Still shining bright like new.
I haven't been a fireman,
For twenty year, or more,
But how my blood still quickens
As they thunder past my door.

So young I was, so very young,
At that old training school,
I climbed the tall hook ladders,
And stayed forever cool.
The daunting heights were nought to me,
I only saw the sky,
I listened to my instructors,
And never reasoned why.
I haven't been a fireman,
For twenty year, or more,
But how my spirit climbs again,
As I did long ago.

I served at Cardiff, Ebbw Vale,
And then at Merthyr town.
Formed friendships deep, and held them long,
And never was let down.
I found what men have found before,
That danger draws the threads,
When flames rise high to tint the sky,
And walls fall past their heads.
I haven't been a fireman,
For twenty year, or more,
Bit I still see the walls fall down,
And hear the bright flames roar.

I met a girl from Middlesex,
And joined the Service there,
Left home and friends, for that true love,
But this I had to bear.
But firemen are sterling souls,
Wherever they may be,
Their strength is steel, their friendship real,
And this they give most free.
I haven't been a fireman,
For twenty year, or more,
But I still feel their manly love,
As in those days of yore.

As they flash by, I look inside,
The cabin where they sit,
To look for those I used to know,
But now no spark is lit;
For comrades fade from Fire Brigade,
As new replaces old,
Though all their warmth through sharing years,
Will never yet grow cold.
I haven't been a fireman,
For twenty year, or more,
But O! how my blood quickens,
As they thunder past my door.

I haven't been a fireman,
For years that form a score,
I haven't heard the bells go down,
They sound for me no more.
I never see the friends I knew,
But knocking on time's door,
Come memories of golden days,
As glorious as before.

~ ~ ~ ~ ~ ~ ~

AFTER HOME RULE

When they passed a law in Cardiff
At the first Welsh Parliament,
That round balls would be banned in Wales,
I wondered what they meant.
For I, who lived in valley deep,
Had seen no other kind
Except the ones shaped like an egg
And made of well tanned hide.

From tender age I'd been brought up
To worship at the feet
Of Rugby Union veterans
Who never knew defeat.
I'd been to countless Rugby games
Accompanied by my Dad,
And cheered on my valley team
With all the breath I had.

Well by the time they passed this law
I must have been quite ten;
And loved the game of rugby more
Than my own countrymen.
Yet being curious, I did ask
Just why round balls were banned,
And did grown men still play with them
In this my native land.

I asked Dai first, as he was old,
And travelled more than most;
For he had left the valley twice,
And even seen the coast.
He hadn't been to Cardigan
Or east beyond the Taff,
But he had seen Llanelli play
When Bennett was fly-half.

I listened then to what he said
That blessed day to me,
As like a forward in a scrum
He hacked me on the knee.

"Son" he said, with quavering voice,
"Yes I have seen the day,
When men in Wales have soccer played,
I am ashamed to say".

"In Cardiff, Merthyr, Swansea too,
And Newport, deep in Gwent,
Unthinking men by bus or train
To soccer matches went.
But when this law was passed at last,
These fools were caught and tried,
And placed in concentration camps
Until their ardour died".

"Now Cardiff City's lost its ground
And Ninian Park its name,
For they have come to see the light
And changed their former game.
While Swansea Town and Newport, Gwent,
With Merthyr Tydfil too,
Now cherish only oval balls,
Just as they ought to do".

On hearing this, I blessed the men
Whose vision was so clear,
And vowed I'd keep the faith with them
To hold the game more dear.
Believing then, as I do now,
That men were born to play,
Not silly games but manly ones
Where brain and brawn hold sway.

So thrilled was Dai by all he said,
That inspiration came,
And taking me to his old ground,
He played his greatest game.
He held me tight against his chest
And ran with heart and soul.
Then twelve yards out he drop-kicked me,
To score a glorious goal.

And if a moral I must point,
Then it must surely be,
That if old men like Dai can kick
Great goals with lumps like me;
Then better far to stick to balls
Egg shaped in these dear vales,
And boot the heathen soccer fans
Completely out of Wales!

~ ~ ~ ~ ~ ~ ~

THE EDGES OF MY DREAM

Scrumping golden russet apples
And the peach soft butter pears
From the orchard that my memory keeps green;
I still watch as ripe fruit topples,
From the bough that groaning bears,
The harvest of the years that lie between.

I can see my brother hiding
From the farmer, in the grass,
As I climbed the weathered trees of long ago.
To send the ripe fruit sliding
Like fat raindrops will down glass,
To recesses in the pillow-case he bore.

Through the misty gateways brimming
From the hopfields past the trees
In the gypsy patterned garments of the day,
Pour the valley men and women
Gaggle waddling like some geese
With their plumage gosling rumpled by the clay.

In the corner of time's murals,
Where my signature I scrawl,
All the colours run together in a stream;
Where like sharp faceted jewels
On the mind's receptive wall
They rainbow light the edges of my dream.

And the apples that we gather
With the melting butter pears
Are windfalls that time's orchard gladly gives
While the guilt child adults father,
With the convict garb it wears,
Is stranger to the innocence that lives.

Turning endless on the ribbon
That is life's Moebius strip
Come the people, joys and places, that have been
Resurrected or unbidden
Where my early footsteps trip
Through the orchards that my memory keeps green.

~ ~ ~ ~ ~ ~ ~

AND GRIEVING CLIMBED

I was valley prisoned once, so may years ago,
And walked slag mountained darkness to the green.
Watched with saddened eyes the slopes, where wild flowers tried to grow,
And grieving climbed to where the air was clean.

Past rusting steelworks, pits, and other graves of man,
Through doors of lifeless houses that were bare.
Tripped by the reddened rails where once steam engines ran,
And listening heard what sounded like a prayer.

Above pond jewelled hollows rose, the sweet gorse prickled hills,
Below, barbed brambled bushes, barred my way.
Where now I walked, once ingots leapt, fire screaming from the mills
And men long dead walked through from yesterday.

A boy I was, a frightened child, my blood sharp spears of ice,
And maggots writhed soft thrusting through my brain.
Afraid to move, my shaking limbs held fast within a vice,
While ancient phantoms walked the world again.

Soiled colliers strode, to long dead pits, from cold disastered tombs,
Their white rimmed eyes framed by the working dust.
Singing they were, in dirge deep tones, from hells own changing rooms
With graveyard hands, in nameless pockets, thrust.

Somewhere, deep doomed, dong bells, through blackened valleys rang,
Their shattering cadences quivering on.
Chime after shocking chime, and clang after brassy clang,
And as their echoes died, the dead were gone.

On twisted branches, tree bound nest bird songsters trilled,
And rising like a whisper from the crest.
The God sweet breeze, through mist choked hollows thrilled,
Then, gently, softly, boyhood flesh caressed.

I came alive within the time that was. The sun
Was golden now, and sucked the moistured air.
Through bladed grass, and fretworked ferns, in foolish fun,
I capered through to where the world was fair.

Since then, I've climbed halfway up life's own mountainside,
And wild flowers picked, that only grow but once.
Struggled through brambled years, scar scratched and torn inside,
I go towards the peaks where darkness hunts.

I was valley prisoned once, so many years ago,
And walked time haunted shadows to the green.
Watched with saddened eyes the slopes, where bright streams tried to flow,
And grieving climbed to where the springs were clean.

NOT ONE OR THE OTHER

This is my once dear Wales, a study
In grey and gold, clear streams and muddy.
Introvert brooding, bright shafts of wit,
Comradeship mined from the depths of a pit.
Hiraeth and hwyl for sale, Bingo and Chapel,
Vanity hatching a worm in the apple
And pride spilling over the National Park
As Wales score a try and a man makes his mark.

This is my once staid street, a bedlam
Of vehicles dogs rush at headlong.
Snarlings of children who endlessly shout
Whispers of old folk who fear to go out.
Doors locked and bolted against hidden dangers,
Neighbours no more but pavements of strangers,
Who nod without smiling and laugh without joy,
As mindless they murder the dreams of a boy.

These are our once proud towns, gilt Eldorados
Schools desecrated by child desperadoes.
Listless flat lagers in face lifted pubs,
Bethels deserted for Sabbath day clubs.
Hymns half remembered from countless revivals
But fuddled by drink and lacking survival
As ghosts of great preachers meet spirits from glass
And in the confusion watch yesterday pass.

This is my nation, not one or the other,
Orphanage Celts without father or mother.
Embracing new cultures that spawned in a void,
Monstrous neurosis undreamt of by Freud.
Hearse-loads of zombies eternally jaunting,
Rushing to nowhere as if to a haunting,
And speaking not Welsh but an English so thin
It slides through the teeth and escapes down the chin.

Here lies the corpse of a Cymru remembered,
Blood drained away and torso dismembered.
Raised from the dead every winter and spring
When men don red jerseys and rugby is king.

Mourn for the caring, the sharing, the hoping,
The hearts that were warm, the doors that were open.
But most of all weep for the children unborn,
Who'll open their eyes to a Wales that's in pawn.

This is my testament, written in sorrow,
Yesterday looking through tears at tomorrow.
Endless horizons of fish and chip hills,
Hamburger vistas and Vallium pills.
Telescoped views of a once glorious people,
Seen from a crypt and not from a steeple,
As blind to the past they get set on their mark
And race without hope from the light to the dark!

~ ~ ~ ~ ~ ~~

AUTUMN'S BREATH

The damsons royal purple lay, night hidden in the trees.
The blushing apples shyly shed their bloom.
The wasp segmented yellow plums were stirring in the breeze,
While space lit stars cast sparks into the gloom.

The swaying hop-bines dressed their ranks, like royal guardsmen will
As soldier like, the nightbirds called the roll.
And ancient oaks, in ordered lines, went marching up the hill,
As if to catch the light that darkness stole.

The rush choked water-lily ponds, night cloaked their teeming life.
The prowling fox drank deep from burnished brook.
The faithful husband soundly slept, his arm around his wife,
And lovers lay replete in shady nook.

The beating heart of mother earth, now drum like stretches skin,
As Autumn's breath fills hollows with its mist.
The rolling hedgerows contours fade, 'neath veils night's spiders spin,
While in the grass, song crickets keep their tryst.

The wasp segmented yellow plums, dew cool their pulpy scars.
The rain sweet earth the orchard trees endow.
The damsons royal purple forms a backcloth with the stars,
And blushing apples sleep along the bough.

MY SAVIOUR SAID

"Touch not these robes", the stranger said
"For these I wore on Calvary's hill,
And all the blood that I once shed
Is soaked into these garments still.
My hands still bear the marks of nails
My brow retains its thorny crown
And God will rent the temple veil
Before men take my body down".

"Move not that stone", the stranger said,
"For I lie dead within that grave,
And I won't rise from that dark bed
Until the world is mine to save.
When eyes will search the eastern sky
For that bright star o'er Bethlehem
And I reborn a baby lie
To bring the gift of life to them".

"Soil not your lips," the stranger cried,
"With promises you can't fulfil,
Twas not for this I hung and died
Upon that cross on Calvary's hill.
I bring my Father's boundless love
To all who walk the way that's true,
For no-one goes to heaven above,
Save by the blood I shed for you".

I looked into the stranger's face,
And stranger was that man no more,
As I reborn at last through grace,
His heavy load of suffering bore.
"Touch now these robes" my Saviour said,
"My wounded flesh your faith has healed,
And move the stone where I lie dead,
That truth might be no more concealed".

And lo! the light of heaven shone
As from His tomb the risen Christ,
The glory of his love put on,
That crown of thorns so greatly prized.
"Touch not His robes" the devil cries,
"Move not the stone that walls Him in"
But much too late, for through Christ's eyes,
We've seen the cross and lost our sin!

~ ~ ~ ~ ~ ~ ~

GOLD GAZOOTS FOR HOPKIN FARR

Hopkin Farr, Dear Hopkin Farr,
What an open book you are.
Rosy, rubicund, and round,
Like an apple, firm and sound.

Twinkling eyes and button nose,
Lungs of brass, we must suppose,
Legs spread out and head thrown back,
The King of Hearts in every pack.

How I loved him long ago,
As to the Carnival I'd go
To see his Spanish Picadors
March like soldiers to the wars.

Flat topped hats and tin gazoots,
Velvet jackets to their suits.
Wide flared trousers graceful fall,
And Uncle Hopkin leading all.

Baton flung up in the air,
Catching hand so debonair.
Evolutions, march performed,
And all Cyfartha Park transformed.

Prizes won and new friends gained,
Childhood magic has remained.
Still I see him from afar,
Lovely Uncle Hopkin Farr.

Hopkin Farr, dear Hopkin Farr,
What a joyful man you are.
May the angels change their lutes
To play you home on gold gazoots.

Hopkin Farr, dear Hopkin Farr,
Heaven's gate is still ajar,
Waiting there for you they are,
With old salutes that sound afar,
On gold gazoots for Hopkin Farr,
Golden Uncle Hopkin Farr.

~ ~ ~ ~ ~ ~ ~

ALL KINDS OF GREETINGS

I hadn't seen Joe for a very long while,
Till we met just by chance in the street.
I flung him a grin and he threw me a smile,
That bounced just in front of my feet.
I tossed him a glance that he fielded with ease,
Then gave him a look that he loathed,
He staggered with this and he fell to his knees,
And rolled on his back in the road.

A 37 bus that for once was on time,
Could do nothing but run over Joe.
I looked at my watch, 'twas a quarter to nine,
(Or perhaps it was twenty past four)
A small crowd had gathered to witness the fun,
So I went round them all with a hat,
Collecting six buttons, an old currant bun
And two dozen fleas from a cat.

Now Joe was as flat as a pancake in pain
(That bus had a bottom and top)
And he slid like an eel through the bars of a drain
('Twas only a thirty foot drop!)
His exit was graceful for he went head first,
So the last things we saw were his toes,
And I cried like a fool as his gall bladder burst,
For this was a favourite of Joe's.

The bus driver groaned (he was late for his tea)
A small spotted dog had a cry.
A wasp that was watching was stung by a bee,
A spider was ate by a fly.
A Siamese cat was chased by a bird,
A Greek squashed a Turkish delight,
And though you might think this is highly absurd,
A West Indian docker turned white.

The crowd had grown larger (and restless as well)
Its appetite wetted by Joe.
For this was a Monday and Mondays are hell,
As every commuter will know.
Like a snail with the gout I rushed to the spot,
And fell on my knees by the drain,
I shook all its bars and I yelled through each slot,
But I rattled and shouted in vain.

The mob, seeking vengeance, came at me with whips
(I saw an assortment of stars)
And I shot down the drain like a panfull of chips,
As they trampled me down through the bars.
It could have been worse as I'm here to attest
For I dropped like a stone upon Joe,
My head broke his leg and my feet smashed his chest,
As he groaned in the darkness below.

In his hospital ward, because he was flat,
They pumped lots of air into Joe.
Whilst I who was chopped up like chips into fat,
Had stitches where I couldn't show.

The moral is clear, when you see an old mate,
Give all kinds of greetings a miss,
Or he could end up as flat as a plate,
And you could be served up with fish!

~ ~ ~ ~ ~ ~ ~

THE BITTERSWEET REMEMBRANCES OF YOUTH

The morning lights the slowly turning world,
Its dawning radiance floods the golden day.
The passing shades of night have heard our prayers,
And God who holds the night has passed our way.
It's now that we remember what He means,
As we recall the days that used to be.
The bittersweet remembrances of youth
To which the glorious Book provides the key.
The feel of Sunday on a summer's night,
The dusty street long shadowed by the sun.
The organ playing hymns to touch the heart,
And old, young, voices fading one by one.
Our friends and neighbours living in our dream,
A different world that will not come again.
When hills around our church were Calvaries,
And every tree a living cross of pain.
The yearly outing to the seaside town,
When fellowship was singing in the sun;
And Saturday was Sunday in the heart,
As burning hymns made bonfires on the tongue.
So as I come repentant to His arms,
My childhood world of faith returns to me,
As innocence remembered in the heart
Transforms the living pages that I see.
The morning warms the slowly turning world,
Its changeless wonder lights the golden day;
And God who holds the night that heard our prayers,
Gives Christ to us, and passes on His way.

THE OLD RUDGE WHITWORH BICYCLE

I pause and see life's melting icicle,
Drip upon drip to the pre-war years,
To see my father's Rudge Whitworth bicycle,
Through memories eyes and a young boy's tears.

Old it was then, but free from all rust,
Sweet lubricated, noiseless as new.
Handlebars shining and frame without dust,
Ready to spin with wheels running true.

Out it would come, shorn of pretensions,
Just like a toy in my father's hands.
His face alight with pride of possession,
Showing the joy a boy understands.

The bike would come from kitchen to hallway,
Eased like a baby through the front door.
To stand at the kerbside defiant and gay;
What I would give to see it once more.

The Aberdare mountain awaited our pleasure,
Girding its loins on the Swansea Road.
The hillside ablaze with the purple treasure
Of wimberries growing where no man had sowed.

Down Darren View flew my father's sweet chariot,
Master astride, and me on the bar,
Basket fine balanced with hand grip to carry it;
Father and son on mission afar.

We leapt the Red Hill like a stallion demented,
Down past Pontmorlais, shaving a tram.
My father said, "sickening", just like he meant it,
I said my prayers and thought of my man.

Ruined old Georgetown gaped at our passage,
This was a cyclist reaching his prime.
A man by the Drill Hall shouted out, "Fascist!"
Escaping our wheels in the nick of time.

Up Swansea Road, more pushing than riding,
Admiring the sounds in my father's chest.
Asthmatic fluid in bronchial tubes hiding,
Some flowing east and some flowing west

I still hear the sweet click of ballbearings turning
Hardly disturbing the hush of the day.
And in the blue sky the golden orb burning
Browning our cheeks from the winter's grey.

Up to the finger-post on the crest stretching,
Pointing the way to Hirwaun and Neath.
Old lorries labouring, taking and fetching,
Alien machines on the upland heath

Here our old friends the Jennings were living,
And here we would leave our old friend on wheels,
Happily walking past green ferns forgiving
The bruising of leaves beneath our hard heels.

Out to the berries on low bushes growing,
And here I remember my dear father best.
Sturdy form bending and ruddy cheeks glowing,
Blessing the earth with a smile and a jest.

Somehow he'd know where ripe fruit grew thickly,
His huge gentle hands like sinuous snakes.
Striking at clusters of berries so quickly,
Making my fumblings look like mistakes.

Time has stood still up there on the dear slopes,
Surely my father is picking there yet.
Love plucks the heartstrings to cherish the lost hopes,
These are the moments I cannot forget.

Forty years on, and still I can see him,
Sitting beside me sharing a meal.
Beloved check cap with unbuttoned brim
Stuck to his curls like an unbroken seal.

Jokes flowed between us, and deep understanding,
For my father knew the heart of a boy.
Posed me no problems his age undemanding,
But taking delight in my boundless joy.

The rest is a dream, for how can words fashion,
The fabric of memories into a whole.
The years pass and with them the heat and the passion
But love for my father stays etched on my soul.

And age is the drip at the tip of the icicle,
Every cold drop is like ice in my brain.
I long for the sight of the Rudge Whitworth bicycle,
With my lovely father astride it again.

~ ~ ~ ~ ~ ~ ~

SHADRACH MORRIS

Shadrach Morris, an uncle of mine,
Short, slim and dark, but erect of line,
Worked as a gentleman's gentleman
At Bourne End, Bucks, till the war began.
Caring for suits of Barons and Lords
Smart tuxedos and Jodhpur Cords,
Shooting jackets and Oxford Bags,
Removing dust and ironing snags.
Polishing shoes till they shone like gems
Where the turned up trousers kissed their hems.
Riding boots as they rose to the knee,
Were dubbined soft as they ought to be.
At his practised touch, with skill innate,
Top hats sprang from their flattened state.
Ties unwrinkled, stretching their silk,
White kid gloves were as virgin milk.
Medical talc in socks was put
To save rich trotters from Athletes Foot.
Collars were pressed till starch complained,
And bow ties arched from knots restrained.

Shadrach Morris was a gift heaven sent,
The perfectly turned out gentleman's gent.

Shadrach Morris, a rookie and raw,
Was ferried east for the Burma war.
Gone the great houses, gone the elect,
Gone were the suits he used to inspect,
Brushing a bush hat, dubbining straps,
Defusing Nipponese booby traps.
Flushed by the Japs, forgetting to jump,
Shrapnel fragmented his tender rump.
Posted to Blighty he swiftly packed
Left buttock gone, but manhood intact.
Uniform mad he returned to Wales,
Post Office trained to deliver mails.

Shadrach Morris, an uncle of mine,
Fond of his pint but steady of line,
As he pushes mail through slotted door.
Thinks of the rich and the clothes they wore,
- But stays in his valley, and valets no more.

~ ~ ~ ~ ~ ~ ~

WHERE SUCH STARS SHONE

Perhaps, you saw it at its best,
This Music Hall of bygone days,
The stand-up comics and the rest,
With patter droll, and funny ways.
The stars who filled the stalls with song,
Without the aid of microphones,
The leopard-skinned young man, so strong,
He cracked with fist, two paving stones.

The Crazy Gang, Nervo and Knox,
Looked down from posters on the walls.
You paid your ninepence at the box,
Or booked a seat in front row stalls.

Perhaps you brought a bunch of flowers,
To throw with love the stage upon,
A tribute to enchanted hours,
That much too soon were dead and gone.

You took into the interval
The simple tunes you heard them croon,
The sweetly played "Me and my gal",
Sung by the Chocolate Coloured Coon.
With glasses raised to thirsty lips
You quaffed light ales and potent wine,
Whilst old men raised their brandy nips
To silent toast the form divine.

The second half of sparkling bill,
Provided stars of magnitude,
And we've gone on applauding still,
In memory those jokes so rude,
Those conjurors whose sleight of hand
Deceived the smoke stung smarting eye,
And gorgeous girls whose beauty fanned
The flames of love, in you and I.

But O! the magic that is gone,
Of those who closed each sparkling show.
Our hearts so warmed where such stars shone,
That we still feel their golden glow.
Perhaps we saw them at their best,
But what a shining best it seems,
That they can reach from where they rest
To weave enchantment through our dreams.

A SOLDIER BOY AM I

I am a full-time soldier boy, a soldier boy am I
I joined because I had no job, I didn't join to die.
Folks say of me I should have known. I know what some folks say,
But they sleep safely in their beds when darkness ends the day.

> CHORUS:
> A soldier boy am I, yes a soldier boy am I
> I just obey my orders and I never reason why.
> A soldier boy is just a man, a man a soldier is,
> The world would be a better place if folk remembered this.

I served in Northern Island, in Ulster did I serve
I saw the bravest blown to bits but never lost my nerve.
I sometimes wonder why I lived, I lived to wonder why
I couldn't find the answer where I saw my comrades lie.

I wed when I was just eighteen, at eighteen was I wed
I wanted love and happiness before they shot me dead.
Folk say I should have waited then, but waiting is for folk
Who think that I'm a number not an ordinary bloke.

I fought down in the Falkland Isles, for Falklanders I fought
I carried out my orders then just like a soldier's taught.
I'm not to proud of what I did, I just did it out of pride,
But when I think of what was done I sometimes cry inside.

There isn't much of life for me, for me there's not much life
There's even less for that sweet girl who is my loving wife.
Though I returned a hero then, no hero can return
Without a mind that's maimed and scarred through watching others burn.

The world is sick of soldier boys, of soldier boys it's sick
But when the bombs begin to fall we're sent for double quick.
They scorn us now but need us then, they need someone to scorn
But when they turn their backs on us we wish that we weren't born.

Some day I'll leave the Khaki ranks, the Khaki ranks I'll leave
I know I'll never lose my stripes but this I'll still believe.
A soldier boy is just a man, a man a soldier is,
The world would be a better place if folk remembered this.

AND THEY LAUGHED

I thought when I spoke to the "Hope" Sisterhood
That my poems were serious and neat
I'd written them over a period of time
When the years and the living were sweet.
I took it as read, that the words that I said
Would be heard with respect as I spoke
Not thinking my verse would be greeted with mirth
As the Sisterhood thought it a joke.

They laughed fit to bust at each word that I said,
They chortled and chuckled with glee.
Grew helpless with laughter and fell off their chairs,
It all looked unnatural to me.
They writhed on the floor, banged their heads on the door,
And some thought their bladders had burst.
As I stood at the front I could hear them all grunt
And I'll tell you I feared the worst.

My nerve broke at last and I started to cry,
I tore out my hair by its roots.
I blushed like a fool (though I'll never know why)
From the crown of my head to my boots.
I stammered and stuttered with each word I uttered
My arms and my legs shook like trees.
While my elbows flew off as I started to cough
And my kneecaps hung down from my knees.

As I spoke my last line I collapsed in a heap,
A pitiful sight to behold.
I brayed like an ass and I bleated like sheep
Who had strayed much to far from the fold.
From my ears could be seen, scalding gushes of steam,
As the water I had on my brain
Boiled away with the heat that came up from my feet,
(For this is the age of the train!)

Well thy gathered me up with the aid of a broom
And a shovel they kept out the back.
I was put in a box though there wasn't much room
And carried away in a sack.

I was buried at sea and they said prayers for me
The very next Sisterhood night,
Though they wonder at times if my verse and my rhymes
Are giving the fishes a fright!

So the moral is plain, if you're speaking quite soon
To Sisterhood meetings in Wales,
You'd be much better off on a trip to the moon
For the Sisters are harder than nails.
They have dug a deep pit which could just be your fit
In a slagheap in Abercwmbach
But they'll hear you out first as they wait for the hearse
And they'll laugh, and they'll laugh, and they'll laugh!!!

~ ~ ~ ~ ~ ~ ~

A BOY WITH A GUITAR

He is a boy with a guitar, but more he is my son,
A tapestry of memories where life's bright dreams are spun.
Evoking music from steel strings that make them sound like gold,
O boy of mine with your guitar, come now my hand to hold.

She is a girl with eyes that melt, but more she's child of mine,
A bridge that like a rainbow spans, the ocean that is time.
A link between two different worlds where men and women care,
O girl of mine with melting eyes, come now my life to share.

She is the woman that I love, but more she is my wife,
A flower opening in the soul, a mother giving life.
Together we have looked at stars, that only lovers see,
O wife of mine, whom I adore, come now to comfort me.

This is the house where we all live, but more it is a home,
Warm flesh around a beating heart that we together own.
With love enclosing our small world, where all in honour trust,
O house of ours wherein we dwell, shut not your doors to us.

These are the words my lips would speak, but more they are not lies,
But true expression of the flame that burns yet never dies.
A feeling that is family, a warmth where blood would flow,
O words of mine that I would speak, come now my love to show!

REFLECTIONS ON HIROSHIMA

Pressed together like two leaves,
But burned by more than Autumn's flame,
Tenderly the earth receives,
These children now without a name.
Takes within it's cold embrace,
A girl without distinctive face,
The boy who's arms had held her tight
To shield her eyes from death's dark sight;
From mushroom clouds that spiralled high,
From atom dust that scarred the sky,
From man's dark cruelty to man,
From scientists who coolly plan,
And juggle molecules of death,
Whilst innocents are drawing breath.

Pressed together like two leaves,
They drift through time to touch the soul;
To haunt the hearts the bomb bereaves,
To point the way to mankind's goal.

Pressed together like two leaves,
The boy and girl without a name,
Tenderly the Earth receives,
And waits with God to set the blame.

STUMBLING THEY GO

Locked behind the lines that time has scored
On ancient faces, lie the prisoners of the flesh.
Unwanted driftwood, suff'ring, lonely, bored,
Their fading, anguished eyes, beseeching tenderness,
Stumbling they go, possessions in their hands,
Through bleak bed sitters' heartless hinterlands.

Perhaps some fought the war to end all wars,
Whilst others manned the nation's merchant ships,
Remembrance Sunday comes, and as we pause,
They wipe the drooling spittle from their lips.
Hapless they go, in some cold Council's care,
With only fading glories left to share.

Some bore the country's sons on beds of pain,
Then saw them march to some forgotten grave.
Twice married women, widowed yet again,
As to a second war their loved ones gave.
Grieving they go, to some small cheap hotel,
And by a spluttering gas fire, go through hell.

The look within their eyes lays bare their souls,
The cruel light of day reveals their shame,
Coats that are frayed, and stockings full of holes,
The weak, the sick, the blind, the deaf, the lame.
Unwanted they sit, on benches in the park,
'Til setting sun leaves old age in the dark.

Through dirty hallways, wraith-like shadows move,
Then wearily to some dark attic climb,
And by unshaded light bulb tread the groove,
Their thoughts have made into the depths of time.
Backward they go, through some old photograph,
Still seeing faces captured in a laugh.

Locked behind the bars that time erects,
The keepers of our conscience wear their chains.
Uncaringly we do what life expects,
And watch their ebbing courage as it drains.
Stumbling we go, to our own dungeon keep,
While young folk in their turn, forbear to weep.

~ ~ ~ ~ ~ ~ ~

YESTERDAY'S SUMMER

When I think back to the music made
By fife and drum in the Boys Brigade
The past comes alive and the present fades
As I march in dreams to the tunes we played.

The quickening step, the shining eye
The long straight road 'neath the summer sky
Lymington Creek and the whistled cry
Of funnelled paddleboats standing by.

Over the gang-plank, marching in droves,
Bell tents, cooking pots, safely stowed,
Cheek by jowl with odiferous stores
Hurricane lanterns and paraffin stoves.

Watching the shore retreating from sight,
Lining the rails in our black and white,
Soaked by spray as the paddle wheels bite,
Churning their way to the Isle of Wight.

And O! the joy as unisoned feet
Thump on the quay to the marching beat
The rumpety tump and the reeds so sweet
Of the drums and fifes in that Yarmouth street.

Vistas of boats on the ebbing tide
As we march in threes with the band inside
Swinging our arms to a lengthening stride
Backs all erect and ramrod with pride.

Ahead, like a promise suspended in time,
Brambles Camp lay at the head of the Chine.
Lips couldn't frame or the senses define
The surge of the blood with the joy that was mine.

Through chinks in the past my memory gleams
Yesterday beckons but never it seems
Will I go back where the paddleboat steams
With its boyish horde to that Isle of dreams.

Oft on the breeze as summer days fade
Bittersweet still come the tunes we played
The rousing strains of the music made
By drums and fifes of The Boys Brigade!

~ ~ ~ ~ ~ ~ ~

TO THE SPIRIT OF TIME

Open my valley with time's rusty lever,
Press back the hills from the riverbed rock
Prise off the roofs of houses and sever
The minutes and hours from yesterday's clock.
Set me with vision on some dreaming mountain,
Then out of the past come deliver to me,
The people and places behind that dark curtain,
That I might bring light and living to thee.

Stretch forth a hand from the flesh of my father,
Rough skinned but warm from the blood in his veins.
Send me his loving and bring me his laughter,
Deliver me strength from the well of his pain.
Set out before me the paths that he followed,
The trust that he carried, the grief that he bore;
Give me his outlook the world never narrowed,
That I might bring light to the living once more.

Bring back the sights and the sounds and the music,
The feel of the earth and the smell of the grass.
Restore to my soul the moments of magic,
So brief in their glory so swift as they pass.
Dazzle my eyes with the mountains spring rainbows
That leapt in their arc the valleys to span.
Take me through time where the wind and the rain goes
That I might bring light to the spirit of man.

Build me a dream from the wonder my eyes saw
When I as a child took my visions to bed.
Mix in the pigments with childhoods raw ochre,
Splash on life's canvas and colour it red.
Bring back my friends from the shadows of twilight,
When singing we walked to the chapel of truth,
Or kneeling in prayer on the meadows of silence,
That I might bring light to the darkness of youth.

O Spirit of Time, past yesterday guide me,
Back to the innocence waiting there still.
Safe in youth's world with my parents beside me,
Warm in my home 'neath the sheltering hill
Set me unfearing on childhood's wild mountain,
Then out of the past come deliver to me,
The untarnished values behind that dark curtain,
That I might see light and the living through thee.

~ ~ ~ ~ ~ ~ ~

KNACKERED

We block booked four chalets at Barry
    That Butlin's great holiday camp
And took all the clothes we could carry
    Twelve wellies, six macs and a gamp.
We came from a number of places
    In England and Merthyr in Wales,
With oil for our bodies and faces
    And spades to put sand in our pails.
We didn't ask much of the weather,
    All places were well within reach,
We wanted to be all together
    In ballroom, theatre, or beach.
Our chalets had bedrooms and kitchens
    For they were self-catering flats;
Baths to keep tropical fish in
    And cracks where they bred the black pats.
There should have been sheets as per brochure,
    Two double for every large bed,

But when we examined them closer
  We found there was just one instead.
Now Idris Ap Daniel, by brother,
  Who almost looked dressed in his clothes,
Put plugs in the ears of our mother
  And swore all his terrible oaths,
Then grabbing my arm he propelled me
  To where the Reception Hall lay.
With many a burp from his belly
  And many a snort on the way.
Red faced he arrived at the counter
  Still holding my arm in his grip,
Calling the desk clerks all bounders
  And cracking his voice like a whip.
"Look here, you dumb oafs" he thundered,
  "It's time you got up off your seats,
We've travelled all day and we're knackered,
  And can't go to bed without sheets!"
Now all of the staff just ignored him
  And dealt with more urgent complaints,
For there were poor husbands reporting
  Great rats who were making wives faint.
Whilst others just asked for removal
  Of wasps' nests from plaster and fridge,
Or maybe the loan of a shovel
  To batter the brains of a midge.
One had encountered piranhas
  Deep down in a lavatory bowl,
Fish who were fond of bananas
  For they were ferociously foul,
And being, by nature, shortsighted,
  They bit what they took to be fruit,
Leaving the victim benighted,
  With less of himself in his suit.
But Idris ignored all this banter,
  Dismissing such cavils as tripe,
And jumping up onto the counter,
  Delivered a speech that was ripe.
"I demand that you give me attention,
  Our grievance must not be ignored.

We're not asking you for perfection,
    But just that our sheets be restored.
Yet you in the face of disaster
    Are dealing with tosh and with tish
Like rats chasing wasps through the plaster
    And flesh-eating piranha fish.
You ought to put things in perspective
    And get your priorities right
By issuing sheets retrospective
    So we can get sleep in the night.
Machine gun the gnats and the midges,
    Feed vampires to piranha fish,
Then put all the rats in the fridges
    For wasps are their favourite dish.
And when all these things are accomplished
    Then you can all call it a day
As with every problem abolished,
    Quite knackered we'll go on our way!"
Well needless to say he was cheered
    By staff and by campers alike,
And even the rats disappeared
    (Though one was seen riding a bike)
And followed by cheering supporters
    We marched to the bed linen store.
With TV newscaster reporters
    Describing the clothes Idris wore.
The cameras their pictures were beaming
    To satellites high in the sky
While fans of my brother were screaming
    With never an eye that was dry.
The sheets we received were redolent
    With Far Eastern pongs that were sweet
Like curry and jungle defoliant
    And scent made from buffaloes feet.
This was a glorious beginning
    With sheets that resembled a sieve.
The absolute cream of their linen
    The finest that Butlin's could give.
We carried them back to our chalet,
    Regaling the crowd as we went

With songs we had heard on the telly
   And jokes writ on walls in the Gents.
Our loved ones embraced us with fervour
   (We'd brought quite a lot in our bags,
It came from a mine up in Merthyr
   Extracted by hand from the slags).
And when we all lay neath the linen
   Recounting the triumph attained
We laughed at the rats in the kitchen
   And listened as midges were brained.
The wasps buzzed in frenzy around us
   Our toilets held piranha fish
But we had our sheets to surround us
   What more could we lucky folk wish!!!

~ ~ ~ ~ ~ ~ ~

DAZZLED BY A VISION OF ANGELS

From the impenetrable reaches of space,
Propelled into the Universe by God's almighty power,
The Jesus star, growing in glory apace,
Moved to its destined place at its appointed hour.

On the dark parched pastures around Bethlehem,
Dazzled by a vision of angels descending to earth,
Humble shepherds, honoured above all men,
Received from the shining host, news of the Royal birth.

From Oriental lands beyond the world's rim,
Drawn as if by a magnet of immeasurable force,
Three men of wisdom, each in himself a king,
Followed the heavenly star back to its earthly source.

From a carpenter's abode in Nazareth,
Directed to Bethlehem, their birthplace, for the census,
Mary and Joseph, seeking a place to rest,
Passed from the ordinary into the marvellous.

Wrapped in swaddling clothes, lying in a manger,
Born to woman impregnated by the Holy Ghost,
A wondrous baby, sent to be a Saviour,
A ransomed Prince that only Heaven could boast.

From the outer perimeter of time and space,
The only Creator that the Universe ever knew,
Following His plan and growing in glory apace,
Stretched forth His mighty hand and angels and star withdrew.

Using the furnace that transmuted the star into a cross,
Illuminating the Scriptures with its imperishable flame,
The burning core of God's devotion, forged from a father's loss,
Changed what was mortal in Man and life without end became.

This glorious unfolding of the Christmas message,
Moving at the speed of love through the awakening mind,
Reveals the blinding truth that man is God's image
And the Son of both is the Saviour of all mankind.

~ ~ ~ ~ ~ ~ ~

SOON MY DEARIE

Listen, lovely, at the dawning,
For the sound of marching feet.
Hear the drums roll through the morning,
Soon, my dearie, we will meet.
How I feel my knapsack lighten,
As my spirits soar on high.
Feel my body muscles tighten,
Where your softness soon will lie.

From the wars are we returning,
From the roar of shot and shell.
From the looting and the burning,
From the very jaws of hell.
From the wounding and the weeping,
From the dying, from the dead,
From the graves where men are sleeping,
In their cold and foreign bed.

See our scarlet tunics blending,
With the wild rose through the grass.
See the clouds of dust ascending,
From that distant mountain pass.
Hear the sweet songs we are humming,
Grace of flute and skirl of pipe,
Through the drumming we are coming,
Where the fruit of life is ripe.

Wait my beauty, where the stream flows,
Where the reeds and rushes rise.
Where your sweet and hopeful dream grows,
Into passion in your eyes.
Make a lover's bed of heather,
Strew wild grasses round your feet,
Soon, oh soon!, we'll lie together,
Flesh to join and be complete.

Look my darling, at the dawning,
Through the fields of golden grain.
See us coming through the morning,
We will not march off again.
Now I feel my musket lighten,
As my spirits soar on high,
Feel my body muscles tighten,
Where your softness soon will lie.

Lovers songs my lips are humming,
Grace of flute and skirl of pipe.
Through the drumming, I am coming,
Where the fruit of life is ripe.

GHOSTS OF OUR CHILDHOOD

I tickled the trout in the pool of the morn
By the light of the dawn's red rays.
The sibilant song of the pebbles was born,
As they fluted the stream of praise.
The icy cold eddies of spring flooded froth
Washed bitingly over my feet,
And I was alive in the turbulent wrath
Where the waters of childhood meet.

I picked with my father the wimberry blush
From the cheeks of the mountain slopes.
Shared summer with him in the fern draped hush
And swam in the pool of his hopes.
Rode crossbar with him on the Rudge Whitworth bike
As we sang to the hum of the wheels,
Freewheeling through pleasure and sadness alike,
Down the hill of my childish ideals.

I walked on a Sunday with family and friends
To the peace of the House of the Lord.
Sharing the vision that our Saviour sends
As we drank of the cup that was poured.
The face of our Minister glowed with the light
Reflected from Bethlehem's star,
That sent us exalted out into the night
Where the ghosts of our childhood are.

Inkstained and bored in the heat of the year
I would gaze through the school rooms' glass
Watching the petals of daffodils stir
As they moved with the wind through the grass,
Seeing not teacher or blackboard or chalk
But paths through the uplands of joy
Where freedom, enchantment and glory walk
Right into the heart of a boy.

So now when I think of the days that are past
The pattern of living unfolds
As sleeping or waking but dreaming at last
I take what the memory holds.

Unbidden but welcome the old phantoms speak
Of the love that was ours long ago,
As if by their telling they hopefully seek
The jewels that yesterday wore.

I walked with my friends to the chapel of truth
In the heat and the cold of the year
Looked through the glass from the school rooms of youth
Where the grass and the daffodils stir
Watched without ending my dear father climb
The wimberry mountains of Spring
And tickled the trout on the finger of time
Where the stones of eternity sing.

~ ~ ~ ~ ~ ~ ~

SHORT FROM THE KNEE

Have you looked at the people who live up in Pant
Whose legs are of differing height,
From constantly walking on hillsides that slant
More to the left than the right?
Have you thought how they felt when they woke up in bed
To know as their legs they did see,
That one of their feet was as far from the head
As the other was short from the knee?

It mattered but little to us or to them
That nature was being denied
Or even that though the world might condemn
They'd nowhere to run to and hide.
So they kept believing the world wasn't round
But angular, awkward and squat.
How else could their left legs be touching the ground
When their right ones were certainly not?

Now this was no trouble while they stayed at home
As the hills they walked on were steep.
But once they had left them and started to roam,
Then they were as lost as their sheep.

For the instant they started to walk on the flat
They all overbalanced and fell,
Which really was awkward for those who were fat
For they were quite helpless as well.

Coach firms in Merthyr ran mystery trips
Which took in the district of Pant
Where those who were witty made merry with quips
When they saw how the hillsides did slant.
Remarking quite loudly to all who might hear,
The legs of the people were such
That if they became quite befuddled with beer,
Twere better to walk with a crutch!

Just how they solved this is talked about still,
As most of you listening have guessed.
For they married people just over the hill,
Whose right legs were longer than left.
Then anxiously waited with long deferred hopes
To prove all the theories right,
That offspring from parents on opposite slopes
Had legs of the very same height.

Of course, as they grew, these children soon found
They couldn't stay upright at all
But tumbled like ninepins on mountainous ground
Down which they rolled like a ball.
And now I am told they have all moved away
To Cardiff and towns that are flat
While Pant is a ghost town where nobody stays
But bedbugs, cockroaches and rats.

So if you are thinking of moving to Pant
Because there are houses to rent.
Just ask yourselves whey they're all built on the slant
And why their inhabitants went.
Then if there's no answer to all that you ask
There's one way this problem to beat.
Just pop down to Merthyr and borrow an axe
Then amputate one of your feet!

~ ~ ~ ~ ~ ~ ~

A DAY OF WONDROUS POWER

It was a blessed moment when this baby girl arrived,
A morsel of humanity, so vibrant, warm, alive.
She fills our very hearts and homes, she means the world to us,
And we are helpless in her grasp, for it was ever thus.

This is a day of wondrous power, for God has blest this child,
Held in the arms of boundless grace, spotless and undefiled.
Of innocence her soul is made, may we help keep it so,
For purity and sweetness reign when evil is no more.

This is the peak of family pride when we to Kathryn give,
The love that springs from wells of joy, as long as we may live.
Her smiles light up the darkest day as if the sun still shines,
And we will all remember this until the end of time.

This is the day we bind with faith, this lovely child to truth,
Not in the tarnished way of age but through the heart of youth.
That she might feel as time goes by, a special link with God,
And walk the shining Way to Life in steps her Saviour trod.

These are the thoughts that heal our minds, the balm that love instills,
The magic power that drives the nerves, the essence love distils.
No words of mine can yet explain just what this baby is,
We can but take the gift she brings and all the love she gives.

There lies the subject of these words, dispensing smiles and tears,
A microscopic part of us, made up of hopes and fears.
We see in her a bright new start, a chance to live again,
To share her wonder and delight, the happiness and pain.

Now is the time to all unite and look through this child's eyes,
To see that place we knew so well, a dream that never dies.
Where people cared much more than now, when values weren't debased,
And hope dear Kathryn finds a world that we as children faced.

Here in this house the future's born, may shadows never fall
Upon this lovely baby girl whose arms embrace us all.
May every hour mean hope fulfilled, may her tomorrows be
As happy as these early days she shares with you and me.

This is the day that we have knelt before the throne of grace,
Prayed together from the heart in God's own holy place.
We've tapped the sources of power divine, may this force work through us,
Dear Kathryn needs the strength we give, for it was ever thus!

Written in love for my Granddaughter's Dedication,
Sunday 19th January, 1986

THE ROCK THAT HE IS

A brother is ore that you mine from the depths, of a shaft that is sunk in the soul.
A metal transformed by the stream of your love to a nugget of glittering gold.
He fits into place in the scheme of your life, like a piece from a jigsaw plan.
First during childhood when you need him most, and then later on as a man.
He's there to protect you from bullies and fools, no matter their size or their weight,
Adoring the people and places you love, detesting the ones that you hate.
Sometimes you quarrel, perhaps come to blows, but this is a storm in a cup
For when you are down he is sorry at once and picks you so tenderly up.
A brother is strength in the grasp of a hand, a brother is friendship that grows.
The armour of righteousness shielding you from all of life's
                                                    indiscriminate blows.
Everyone of your needs he will try to fulfil, he knows not what selfishness means,
And longs to be wanted by your wayward heart and to share in your
                                                    hopes and your dreams.
He never quite knows what your view of him is for words can't
                                                    express what you feel,
But takes it for granted his love is returned, no matter how
                                                    much it's concealed.
A brother is prop when the weight of the world seems to bear on
                                                    your shoulders alone,
A crutch for your lameness, a guide for your steps, a brace to each
                                                    muscle and bone.
A stiffening of sinew to face what you must, the world isn't always your friend,
And so he finds time, in the heat of his youth, to come to your side and defend.

No setback deters him, no odds are too great, he never takes quarter from pain,
But gives of his all, with his last ounce of strength, not once, but again and again.
A brother is someone who sleeps in your bed when you're small and
                                                    your family is big,
Burying your secrets in night's sombre grave as together dark's tunnel you dig.
Whispering of ghosts through the creakings of night, yet there with
                                                    a steadying hand
As the house, which is old, settles down on its beams and its timbers
                                                    contract or expand.
He'll go down the stairs just to fetch you a drink, though the dark
                                                    makes his spirits quail,
Fearfully treading on murmuring boards as he clings to the bannister rail
He simply believes beyond question of doubt, that his life's interlocked
                                                    with your own,
A singing of blood in the veins of one flesh from the seeds of your parents grown.
A feeling of family, founded on pride, determined to face life and win,
As those without hope turn faces to wall, as the forces of darkness close in.
A brother is silver you find in your hand when the cash in your pocket has gone,
A cigarette offered which might be his last, a rightness when everything's wrong.
An arm round your shoulders each time that you're hurt, a hankie to
                                                    wipe away tears,
A voice that is warm through the days that are cold, in the ice of your
                                                    formative years.
He always instinctively says the right thing, when your mind is
                                                    bedevilled by doubt,
Giving advice that is balm to your soul, for he knows what you worry about.
A brother is shouting that echoes through time, laughter that thunders with joy,
Companionship shared when a boy feels a man, and a man is no more than a boy.
Standing with you on the pitches that slant as the team you support gives its all,
And racing you down the precipitous slopes as you rush to recover a ball.
But more than all this, is the unspoken love, that is never referred to by name,
Lapping like waves on the shores of your heart, but never extinguishing flame,
That will burn in you both, for as long as you live, a light that won't
                                                    flicker or fade,
Until you set out on that long lonely road, where the final great journey is made.
And so you give thanks for this brother of yours, and pray that
                                                    he'll always be there
So when love's foundation is laid in the heart, the rock that he is will be there!

A VALLEY WEDNESDAY

It was a valley Wednesday, the mountains looked quite bleak
As I gazed from my railway coach, to where I was to speak.
The Parish Church stood clearly out, and in its shadow there
I saw the roof that God had built, set firm on Market Square.

I knew the rain would soon come down, I'd seen the signs before,
The darkened skies, the mountain mist, the load the stormclouds bore.
I thought of all the elderly who hoped to come and share
An evening with their Lord and me, down there in Market Square.

The world around went on its way, for who was there to know
That through a quiet backstreet church, great streams of mercy flow.
And those who braved the elements, found God had time to spare,
To listen to their inmost thoughts in Merthyr's Market Square.

I looked at each expectant face and hoped that I could give
A message that would lift their hearts, a promise that would live.
For I was but the instrument and speaking through me there,
Was One much greater than myself or those in Market Square.

My talk was interspersed with verse, for God bequeathed to me
The poet's gift that shines dull words and sets the spirit free.
With these I built a Christian home on rock that gladly bears
A temple such as that dear church that's known as Market Square.

The words were stored within my mind and burnished with the truth
And spoke of dear, sweet, family days I knew of in my youth.
Of mother, father, children, wife, who make my world so fair
That only God knew how I felt, back there in Market Square.

Christ washed his twelve disciples feet, the words were His, not mine.
Yet I was moved beyond all else, by this one act divine.
For if our Lord could do this thing to show how we must care,
Then this example lights the world, not only Market Square.

So on the everlasting rock, a Christian home I built,
Its bricks held fast by mortar made from blood our Saviour spilled.
The roof was firmly set in place, the rooms were filled with prayer
That we had offered up to God, that night in Market Square.

It was a valley Wednesday, but Jesus changed all that,
As I looked down from where I stood to where my listeners sat.
The Parish Church was near by, but here where people share
I saw the home that God had built for us in Market Square.

~ ~ ~ ~ ~ ~ ~

'PON MY SOUL

So careful and slow, I measured the dose,
Dripped all the drops, and sniffed with my nose.
Added some acid and fine powdered glass,
Gave it some bubbles with CO_2 gas.
Stirred with a spoon that was silver and old,
Poured in a goblet of finely wrought gold.
Placed in a dark, spidered, cellar to age,
Cast o'er it a spell of dark passioned rage.
Put round it a circle of anthracite coal,
Then waited for he who would come for my soul.

The Devil came for me, before I was dead,
Cast shadows of fear to darken my bed.
Asked for some wine while he waited for me,
Rubbed hard horny hands and cackled with glee.
I sent my good servant to fetch him the dose,
The Devil, expectant, came up to me close,
And drinking the poison, with pleasure did roar,
"Hells bells, that was lovely - please give me some more!"

~ ~ ~ ~ ~ ~ ~

THE THING

The waves slunk back to the ebbing sea,
To the wail of the curlews call.
The desolate sky looked down on me,
As I sat by the harbour wall.
The rotting boats, past high tide mark,
Barnacled, blistered and bent,
Dreaming perhaps of the deep sea shark,
And the old Spice Island scent.

I carried a spy glass in my hand,
For the long and studied stare.
I looked to the gold and furrowed sand,
Though my mind was past caring where;
And saw where the hissing wavelets fled,
Full bloated, decaying, obscene,
A man like shape with monstrous head,
And scaled with an emerald green.

The day was young, and the town's folk slept,
And I was alone on the shore;
Feeling a chill as the terror crept,
From my heart to my inmost core.
Trembling I walked to the magnet drawn,
Like a man to his fresh dug grave,
My staring eyes on the devil's spawn,
Death kissed by the last wild wave.

Around my neck on a fine spun chain,
Was my mother's own cross of gold,
And I felt it's fire burning my brain,
Though my feet and my hands were cold.
My footsteps led, where the sand crabs dredge,
Past the rocks where the shellfish cling,
Until I stood at the water's edge,
Alone with the awesome thing.

A full nine foot it measured out there,
And humanoid was it in form.
Its feet were shod, but the body lay bare,
Though the emerald scales were warm.
It lay on its back, with despairing arms,
Appealing perhaps to the sun.
With eye like the clay that the yeoman farms,
For the creature had only the one.

There were no ears, just two small holes,
Sunk deep in the sides of the skull.
A shark-like mouth with teeth like coals,
Jet black like a fire scarred hull.
One of its hands, full webbed and clawed,
Was balled like a huge clenched fist,
Holding a scroll, fast bound with cord,
And covered with outlandish script.

I fell to my knees and gently took,
From a hand that had waved at Mars,
The parchment roll like an ancient book,
That had come from the distant stars.
I gripped and tugged as the knot untied,
And I starred at the unrolled scroll,
While the words within, lived once, then died
As they branded themselves on my soul.

The Thing had come from the distant rim,
Where the universe touched to the void.
Where space was black and the stars shone dim,
And the living energy boiled.
Its ship had sped through chartless space,
At speeds much faster then light,
Bringing the word to the human race,
That it faced an endless night.

The ancient seers, on that far flung world,
Calculating the death of the suns,
Where hydrogen flared and molecules hurled,
Like the roar of a billion guns,

Had seen from figures, computers spun,
That the stars in our own night sky,
Would all go nova one by one,
As their molten hearts ran dry.

The messenger sprawled in its slimy pool,
While compassion stirred in my heart,
The sweat drops formed though my brow was cool,
For I felt like a man apart.
Entrusted with secrets the world knew not,
Though knowing was torture to me,
And wond'ring why it befell to my lot,
To unravel the mystery.

The cross of gold I was fingering still,
As I cast my mind through the years.
When a lonely man on a distant hill,
Had died to the multitudes' jeers.
Two thousand years of the Light that shone,
Now a long return to the dark,
The reckoning come, and the Kingdom gone,
Not leaving the faintest spark.

The rosy glow of the dawn's first flush,
Was deserting the eastern sky.
The first faint sounds broke the morning's hush
As the waking hour drew nigh.
I offered a prayer of my deepest wish,
As I saw as a prophet sees,
The long doomed men as they cast for fish,
In the waters the morrow would freeze.

Nothing could hinder that judgement day
And knowledge would cause only pain.
I walked to the store where the petrol lay
Then back to the creature again.
I emptied the spirit all over its scales,
And lit with a hand tossed match.
The head went first, then the clawlike nails
'Til it burned to an empty patch.

The waves slunk back to the ebbing sea,
To the wail of the curlews call.
The desolate sky looked down on me,
As I walked to the harbour wall.
The sun was red and edged with fire,
And I grieved for my alien friend,
My sombre thoughts on the funeral pyre,
As I waited with God, for the end.

~ ~ ~ ~ ~ ~ ~

A MAN OF PEACE

"Now", said Morgan Talbot Rees,
(Giving us his party piece)
"Scrum down tight against their eight,
Use your elbows, use your weight.
Strike like lightning 'gainst the head,
On their insteps savage tread.
Channel back to Dai the Scrum,
Let the ball to our backs come.
Dummy scissors to the right,
(I've been told they're not that bright!)
Take your passes on the burst,
Flatten their flank forwards, first.
If you see their full-back pause,
Forget about the rules and laws,
Knock him flat while Islwyn Coates,
Touches down between the posts".

"Now", said Morgan Talbot Rees,
Surplice on, a man of peace,
"Help me up on these pulpit stairs,
Time it is to say our prayers.
Peace on earth, goodwill to men,
Bless us Lord of Hosts, Amen!"

~ ~ ~ ~ ~ ~ ~

THE PATIENT HORSE.

So strong, so brave, the patient horse,
Man's friend through countless centuries;
By harness scarred, and cut by spurs,
A beast, perhaps, but nothing worse,
For man he lives, by man he dies.

His usefulness has come and gone,
No more the plough or river barge.
No more broad backs to sit upon,
No more brave knights whose armour shone,
Or thund'ring hooves in battle charge.

On him we dreamed our oldest dreams,
As man rode through time's early dawn,
Swam side by side through virgin streams,
And harnessed him to wagon teams,
To cart the sheaves of ripened corn.

So strong, so brave, in all his ways,
Man's friend and transport through the years,
In sport our partner, and in chase,
It's we, not he, that know disgrace,
And he, not we, deserve the tears.

~ ~ ~ ~ ~ ~ ~

AFTER THE GALA

After the Gala the streets were dead
And dark slid down the wimberry hills.
Small boys followed their dreams to bed
And lovers lay with the daffodils.
The segment moon in its cumulus shrouds,
Crescent horns tossing the matador stars.
Tore like a bull through rowelling clouds
As night owls hooted their muted hurrahs.

After the Gala, the jazz bands sat
In pubs, still dressed in their marching suits,
Velvet flares and Picador hats
And rousing tunes on their tin gazoots.
The kettledrum lads like make believe men,
Strutting behind their buttons of brass,
At chucking out time on the stroke of eleven
Rolled with the girls in the mountain grass.

After the Gala, the Fancy Dress prize
Went to a beggar arrayed as a King,
While Arab and Negro (colliers disguised)
Mined the burnt cork from pits in the skin.
Daredevil Jack on his one sound leg,
Fresh from this dive from the heights in the park
Tapped with his stick and stumped with his peg
Out of the light and into the dark.

After the Gala the discarded clown,
Eyes laid to rest in the grave of his face,
Cried in his room at the edge of the town
Mourning the death of his Carnival days.
The sideshow attendants, customers gone,
Tents packed away with the coconut stands,
In caravan caves where Tilley lamps shone,
Counted their pennies with Diddicoy hands.

After the Gala, the world's strongest man,
Arms racked by spasms of muscular pain
Sat in his lodging house trying to cram
Mountains of food in a mouth like a drain.
The bearded lady, troubled by fears
That interest in her was beginning to fall,
Nourished the roots of moustaches with tears
And tortured by doubt turned her face to the wall.

After the Gala the cleaners arrived,
Shocked to the core by the state of the park.
Close to despair as the litter defied
All their attempts to clean up by dark.

Tellers of fortunes their palms silver crossed,
Crystal balls packed in their boxes of tin,
Walked through the alleys bewildered and lost
Not knowing what all their tomorrows would bring.

After the Gala young children dispersed,
Tears streaming down from eyes that were sore.
Some to be scolded, some to be nursed,
Some to remember this day evermore.
Sing for the joy their little minds treasured,
Mourn for the warmth their grieving hearts missed.
Dreams such as these can never be measured,
Or all the wonders these tender ones wished.

After the Gala, the lake in the park,
Boats rocked to sleep on its silvery bed.
Tucked all its rushes away in the dark
And folded its ripples on shores that were dead.
The corpulent swans, heads buried in breasts,
Gracefully etched in the shadow of trees,
Conveyed their cygnets to feathery nests,
Moving together with effortless ease.

After the Gala the trapezists lay,
(Star spangled still in their glittering tights)
Warm with their women in Pandy Farm hay,
Soaring through sleep to impossible heights.
The river Taff rolled past the Pontsarn ridge
Bearing its silver on platters of trout,
The mirror clear pools by the Cefn bridge
Reflecting the sparks as the stars came out.

After the Gala when I was a boy,
The fields in the park were darkened and still,
And I walked home through a valley of joy
To my childhood world at the top of the hill.
My mind is the river where memories pour,
My soul comes refreshed from its glittering streams;
And though I may go to the Gala no more,
Through sleep come the clowns in remembering dreams.

REFLECTIONS ON ABERFAN

They might have been autistic, but this they never were,
Thalidomide or Spastic, a cross too hard to bear.
They could have been brain damaged and lost beyond recall,
But these were healthy children and the black dust took them all.

The future years were waiting, but the hours slipped by in vain,
Their talents undeveloped but not their parents' pain.
Many roads their feet might tread lead now to loneliness,
And mothers' arms that reach through time, find no-one to caress.

It's other peoples youngsters now whose echoes catch the breeze,
Yet piping cries o'er childrens graves will never waken these.
The brooding slag has gone for good, yet some eyes never see
The seasons change on mountainside or leaves fall from a tree.

In valley chapels, silent prayers, still death's dark valley span,
Perhaps to where their children play, beyond the reach of man.
Or maybe sunbeams stained by glass come shafting through the rain
To sombre bathe the mourners in the colours of their pain.

From Dowlais Top to Quakers Yard, the Merthyr valley grieves,
Forgetting not the downy heads that dream beneath their wreaths.
Remembering still each eager face, each smile and childish tear,
And seeking hope where hope must lie, beyond the reach of fear.

Time will heal the hillside scars, pray God it heals us all.
The past is done, the future waits where leaves of memory fall.
For Aberfan like Calvary is part of mankind's loss,
To bear like Someone greater bore, the burden of our cross.

HEARD NOT THE CHOIR

Have you heard of our choir from Abercwmgravy
Who went down to Portsmouth to sing for the Navy?
We set off expectant by dawn's early glow
From mountains and hills where the wimberries grow.
We carried twelve cases of Rumney strong ales,
Pork pies and faggots and cockles from Wales.
Beetroot, red cabbage, with brown bread and white,
Trifles and seedcake to blow , suck and bite.
Jars full of gherkins to give us a thirst
And practice for songs that we hadn't rehearsed.
We didn't take women - not even my Gran,
Except for Blod Morgan who sang like a man.
Women are foolish and chatter too much,
Distracting good talk about rugby and such.
They get in the way and they try to talk posh,
Nibble sweet biscuits and polish off squash.
Sweethearts and mistresses, wives by the score,
They once rode beside us but never no more.
There's stupid I felt when my own Mary Jane
Took pills with some brandy when flying to Spain,
And tried to force open the door in the side
Convinced she had wings to hover and glide.
It took all the tact of the whole cabin crew
To try to persuade her that only birds flew!

So now we were off, a rampant Welsh choir,
Our heads in the clouds and our bellies on fire.
Ale swiftly flowing from bottle to glass
Through stomach to bladder in bubbles of gas.
Pork pies to crumbs and faggots to wind,
Beetroot de-jarred and the gherkins unskinned.
Trifles ignored in their waxed paper shells,
Seed cake remembered but only in spells.
Danny Full Pelt who was driving our bus
Drove with one hand as he drank ale with us.
He weaved lovely patterns across all three lanes,
Leapt level crossings in front of the trains.

Left his seat twice as he came back for more,
Went to the exit and slid back the door.
Cheerfully waved to the drivers of cars,
Lifted his elbow and had a few jars.
With nobody driving the bus went alright,
Safer in fact with our Danny so tight.
Somebody said "We have just gone through York",
But he was soon calmed and treated for shock.
Hearing a siren I looked through the glass
To see two police cars were trying to pass.
Danny Full Pelt who was standing nearby
Swallowed a gherkin and started to cry.
"It's all over, Boyos" he whimpered to us
"Those flamers are rozzers and chasing my bus".
He ran to the front and jumped on his seat
And drove the wrong way up a One Way Street.
Fair play though for Danny, he didn't mean harm,
He couldn't help hitting that furniture van.
Pork pies went one way and ales by the score
Jumped from their cases and smashed on the floor.
Blodwen had faggots all over her skirt
Trifles exploded, but no-one was hurt.
Red cabbage scattered in one gory flood,
Half of us fainted, we thought it was blood!
Seed cake in wedges just flew through the air
But no-one complained they weren't getting their share.
The seats broke like matchwood, the whole roof caved in
And Prosser the Post had my foot on his chin.

It took fifteen hours to cut through the steel
And Danny Full Pelt who was stuck to his wheel
Was pulled by his hair through the hole that was made
By rozzers in blue and the fire brigade.
No sooner outside than the Chief of Police
Charged us with causing a breach of the peace.
Still, there is lovely we sang in the cells,
"Myfanwy", "Cwm Rondda" and "Dances with Elves".
But thinking about it we all had to smile
We'd set of for Portsmouth and this was Carlisle.
Sufficient to say that the boys of our Navy,
Heard not the choir from Abercwmgravy!

A MAN IS NOT

A man is not and never can be part of a machine,
For how can soulless metal know the joy the eye has seen.
The cutting edge a handle moves makes shapes from turning steel
But none so lovely as the forms the dreaming mind reveals.

A thought is not and never can be reproduced at will
Although computers fed by man can easier tasks fulfil.
We watch aghast as relays click and endless figures pour
And think with minds God gave to us, that we can take no more.

A soul is not and never will be more than man's blind faith,
Unseen by mortal human eye, yet in a state of grace.
A vessel so receptive that it holds within its shell,
That means to inward grow to God and in His mansions dwell.

A heart is not and never can be standard like a pump,
For blood, not oil, is forced through valves from deep within its sump.
The nervous system of the brain affects its every beat,
A heart is vibrant, living warmth, not just a piece of meat.

A smile is not and never can be mirror to the soul,
Unless the joy that fuels it can make the spirit whole.
Luminance such radiance casts, moves shadows from the night,
While all whose lives are touched by it are grateful for its light.

A brain is not and never can be serviced like a car
Though there are some psychiatrists who force its doors ajar;
But those who would explore its depths with maps that man provides,
More blindly into unknown worlds on paths where darkness hides.

A prayer is not and never will be listened to by God
Unless we come to Him through Christ and walk the paths He trod.
No easy bypass winds past faith, the cross still bars the way
And we must take His body down, before we kneel to pray.

A life is not and never can be more than just a page,
Although the book that holds it fast might last from age to age;
Yet printed there in blood not ink, the story that unfolds
Is comedy and tragedy that crowded living holds.

A man must be by reasoning, much greater than machines,
As moved by love, reborn through faith, his soul the heart redeems.
He comes through prayer and deep belief to see the world through eyes
From whence the veil of darkness lifts, to point him to the skies!

~ ~ ~ ~ ~ ~ ~

FOR DANNY LOOKS

I have two brothers and love them both,
For Danny looks from each.
They smile his smile, and wear his cloth,
Of gentleness in speech.
I hear their voices, loving, warm,
And know there is no death,
As my dear father, strong and calm,
Speaks through their every breath.

The hand that writes this, his love bore,
The words are his and mine.
And with my brothers we are four,
Immortal in our line.
Our sons are his and he is them,
For they all bear his name,
And outward grow from that straight stem,
From whence his loving came.

O Danny, Danny, were you here,
To see with this worlds eyes.
Your pride would be, a tender tear,
Your joy a hearts surprise.
Your two strong hands that worked for us,
Would Benediction give,
And hold us all with hope and trust,
As long as we all live.

We bear his name, and we are proud,
To be what he would choose.
To think his thoughts and shout aloud,
The joy our hearts can't lose.

The upland hills that knew his tread,
Are monuments to him,
For while they stand he be not dead,
Nor does his light grow dim.

And we three brothers stay entwined,
For Danny's in our eyes.
We have his heart, his soul and mind,
For loving never dies.
And when our grandsons, yet unborn,
Can smile through grief and pain,
We'll know where our dear father's gone,
As Danny lives again.

~ ~ ~ ~ ~ ~ ~

GONE FROM HENCE

The barns are empty now, that housed
The valley folk. The vast bell tents
And straw snipped, rat gnawed huts where groused
The sing song tongues, have gone from hence
To secret places where they rot unseen.
The corrugated iron sheds
Where meals were cooked on braziered fires
Shelter no more hop pickers heads
Or trembling quake to ringing choirs,
But stand mildewed, odiferous, unclean.

The barbed wire fence that kept our flesh
From orchard fruit, still holds upon its spears
Fine shreds of skin, no longer fresh,
But rotted yellow by the festering years
That separate us from eternal trees.
Dreamlike I totally recall
The endless chases by the farmer and
His men of scrumping women, small
Boys and the fearing, chattering band
Of girls, with tresses flowing in the breeze.

The canvas of the cribs that bore
Our hops, still serves a purpose, by
Draping and protecting the more
Exposed corners of the bines.
My Heart trembles at this, remembering the white
Frost, late in September, stabbing honed
Knives through the early mist, that cut
Into fingers until the fine boned
Hands tingled as if shrieking shut
In the slammed door of yesterday's night.

Even the trains that transported
Us to Withington and Ledbury
Are different now, being coated
In the Western Region livery,
That evokes praise but not admiration.
Perhaps the trains still run on rails,
Endlessly tracking through memory,
Curving forever outward from Wales
Into a Herefordshire timelessly
Sprouting hops that await liberation.

They can't inter machines that die,
Like the frail flesh of the people who
Also stripped the hops. And yet by
Some trick of nature the machines do
Oxydise until they stand like skeletons.
To muse on this and to remember
The blessed good in the very bad
Days, is to relive each September,
That golden with promise and yet sad
With an ache that blinds us to the elements,
Makes us at one with nature and slots the
Hopfields of our youth into Welsh valleys,
Where heart and soul, not mind, work out the measurements.

~ ~ ~ ~ ~ ~ ~

MEGAN (Five Pints)

Each morning, for her Guinness,
She comes - oh yes she comes
Her manner bright and skittish,
Her coat festooned with crumbs.
She wears an old Victorian hat
With artificial plums;
Primed for her early morning chat,
She comes - oh yes! she comes.

She seems to float on alcohol
And oozes through my door
She never lets me down at all
But always comes for more.
Her wicker basket bumps on wheels,
Just like the sound of drums.
On pallid legs, like jellied eels,
She comes - oh yes! she comes.

She owns to being eighty-three
But I would take a bet,
That you could add ten years and be
As near as you could get.
She buys cheap pints and not dear halves,
She's clever with her sums.
In lace-up boots that hide her calves,
She comes - oh yes! she comes.

She drinks five sticky pints a day
Within her small front room;
But still emerges bright and gay,
Like potted plant in bloom.
At some rude jest she'll cackle loud,
Displaying toothless gums,
And pushing basket through the crowd,
She comes - oh yes! she comes.

One day I know she'll not appear,
Though stout flows through her veins.
I'll miss her alcoholic leer,
Her coat with beery stains.
On spirit Guinness she will float
While angel choir hums;
In wicker basket like a boat,
She comes - oh Lord! she comes.

AND THE WAY IS THE LIFE

I have walked this road to the source of life,
With my boy and girl and my lovely wife,
Through the days of peace and the days of strife,
Have I walked this road to the source of life.

I have known great love, I have felt deep pain,
Through the fields of hope I have marched again,
To that far green hill where our Lord was slain,
For a greater love and a deeper pain.

I have strayed at times, when the road was rough,
When my body has screamed, enough!, enough!,
But then I have looked to the heavens above,
And the straying ceased though the road was rough.

I have heard from the lips of godly men,
That the faith was reborn at Bethlehem,
That the angels spoke to the shepherds then,
Through the lips of God, to the souls of men.

I have swallowed dust from a thousand feet,
As I followed the cross through burning heat,
To the place of skulls where the world's roads meet,
But the Lord was there, and the dust was sweet.

I have watched the sun, as its last red rays,
Reflected blood from the body of praise,
And the light of His love as it shone from His face,
Lit the circle of thorns o'er His Kingly gaze.

I have learned through Him, that worldly things,
Mean nothing without what the gospel brings,
And the Christian poor are greater than kings,
In the vaults of heaven where His glory rings.

I have found my tree in the forest of truth,
Where the roots go deep with the strength of youth,
And the faith in its stem is compounded of proof,
In the tree of our Lord, in the forest of truth.

I have walked this road to the source of life,
With my boy and girl and my lovely wife,
Through the days of peace and the days of strife,
And the road is the Lord's, and the Way is the Life!

~ ~ ~ ~ ~ ~ ~

PERSONAL TESTAMENT

I write of a time that my heart knows best,
I write of the days that are gone.
I speak of the hours that love has blessed,
As the days go moving on.
I weep and I laugh, know sadness and joy,
As I see what the past unveils.
And I am alive in the heart of that boy,
Who grew up in the valleys of Wales.
I walk again with the friends that I knew,
Up slopes that climbed to the sky,
Where we stood like gods in the evening dew,
And watched the long days die.

Where we talked of matters beyond our ken,
Galaxies spinning in space.
Or solved again in the manner of men,
The problems besetting our race.
That strange sweet love that was felt by us all,
Bound us with magical chains,
And brothers we were who answered the call,
Of the blood that flowed through our veins.
The valley was dark as the sun went down,
Except for the distant lights,
Festooning the streets of that dreaming town,
Back there in the prewar nights.
Or the pattern of lamps on the twisting roads,
As they lighted the colliers' way,
In buses that came with their weary loads,
At the end of each working day.
Who can recapture the feel of the times,
That golden mysterious taste;
Or brush the green fern as the memory climbs,
Up slopes that our footsteps graced.

The chalk scented days in the old Infants' School,
The toys for the afternoon games.
The serious child and the usual fool,
The baiting and calling of names.
Hymns that were sung from the throats of the young,
At the start of each babbling day.
The grazes that throbbed as the iodine stung,
As we tumbled in childish play.
O may I know the sweet pain of it all,
O may life's shadow disperse.
Turn back the clock on the schoolhouse wall,
The pattern of life to reverse.
Sing from the soul all the old childhood hymns,
The Lord let my shepherd be.
Stand me again where the memory dims,
That I might be privileged to see,
The days that are gone that burned like a flame,

Scorching the edge of life.
The reading of scripture in God's holy name,
That pierced our hearts like a knife.
The making of swords for the Infant School plays,
Excalibur lifts from the lake.
And I am King Arthur in those ancient days
Who cares if the sword is a fake.

Who knows where the dream and reality meet,
Who reads all the thoughts of a child.
Who dares take away all the joys bittersweet,
That age in these days has defiled.
Who is there living can say what is truth,
The cloak of expediency falls,
And we must return to the days of our youth,
To breach insurmountable walls.
To force our way back to all that was good,
To decency, honour, and love.
To stand once again where innocence stood,
And to know that this is enough.
The sins of the world would all slough away,
And purity reign in their place,
While childhood triumphant rememb'ring to pray,
Would conquer the final disgrace.

Yes, deep in the valley the cradle still stands,
And each generation renews,
The hopes and fears mankind understands,
A gift for the future to use.
Time passes, we age, with our tarnished ideals,
Still yearning for all that is lost,
Not seeing that place where a tender child kneels,
Or the rivers of pain that we've crossed,
We come from our valleys, forsaking what's ours,
Those roots that are one with the soil.
We follow our star as the bright vision sours,
And all that we touch seems to spoil.
We long for the sound of the soft lilting tones,

That echo all Wales through our hearts;
The sense of belonging that lives in our bones,
The lesson that History imparts.
We stand to be counted with those who remain,
To find our bright visions reborn,
The dark fades away and we see once again,
The promise that follows the dawn.

I write of the time that my heart knows best,
I write of the days that are gone.
I speak of the hours that love has blessed,
As the days go moving on.
I weep and I laugh, know sadness and joy,
As I see what the past unveils,
And I am alive in the heart of that boy,
Who grew up in the valleys of Wales.

BIOGRAPHICAL NOTES

Ray Harman was born on June 27th 1922, the son of a steelworker in Penyard, Merthyr Tydfil, Glamorgan. He received his education, first at the Queen's Road School and later, after passing the eleven plus examination, at the County School in Penydarren.

He joined the RAF at the start of the second world war, serving both at home and in the Far East and, on demobilisation, enrolled with the National Fire Service. After an intensive fire fighting course he served as a fireman in Ebbw Vale, Cardiff and Merthyr Tydfil. Later he transferred to the Middlesex Fire and Ambulance Service after meeting his future wife ,Dorothy, who resided in that county.

Ray has been writing poetry from an early age and much of his work has been influenced by being born into a coal mining family which saw six of its members die, either through accidents underground or from dust related lung diseases.

He has performed on stage with Victor Spinetti, Glyn Houston, Stan Stennett, Lewis Jones, Mari Griffiths and many more well known Welsh entertainers - all of whom have placed on record their admiration for his work. Even Max Boyce has phoned Ray at home requesting copies of his poems and has been kind enough to say that "How can you tell" is his particular favourite.

Much of Ray's work has been published and all of his poems which have been featured on television are included in this collection.

He has been happily married for forty-three years, has two married children (a son and a daughter) and five cherished grandchildren. He is a lifelong Christian and worships at the Ashford Congregational Church. He lists his hobbies as poetic composition, modern sequence dancing and babysitting his beloved grandchildren. Now, seven years into his retirement, Ray is busier than ever, and who knows what fresh fields he might yet set out to conquer!

Recent books by Horseshoe Publications:

WATER UNDER THE BRIDGES by Freda Price

In this nostalgic and evocative saga centred in the Cheshire town of
Runcorn, Freda Price (a first-time author) has produced a detailed and
sensitive chronicle of family life there from the turn of the century to
present times.

The town's development from a small port to a thriving industrial area was
chiefly due to the cutting of the Bridgewater and Manchester Ship Canals
through it, which not only permitted easy transportation of raw materials
to aid the introduction of local tanning and chemical industries, but also
resulted in the influence of men and women from Liverpool, Manchester
and many other North Western parts of the country.

Against this background, the author outlines the progress of her forebears
through hardship and deprivation and goes on to relate fascinating
accounts of schooldays, varieties of entertainment, job-hunting and so on in
her own time. The trauma of the Second World War, as it affected Runcorn
and surrounding districts, and later changes which culminated in the
town's present semblance, are also portrayed with considerable depth of
feeling.

The combination of Freda Price's easy literary style and Tracy Walkden's
delightful illustrations definitely justifies a place for 'WATER UNDER THE
BRIDGES' on your bookshelf.

In hardback **£10.99**

THE CAT & THE CREAM OF SHORT STORIES AND POETRY
by Cheshire Writers

A collection of entertaining and unusual material written by first-time
writers throughout Cheshire. Compiled by the Editor, John C. Hibbert, this
booklet is the forerunner of a new series of books to be launched in the
New Year under the title 'The Traveller's Friend'.

In laminated softback **£3.50**